MENTAL ILLNESS

2nd Edition

LONDON: HMSO

Applications for reproduction should be made to HMSO Copyright Unit, Norwich NR3 1PD
Third impression 1996

ISBN 0 11 321829 X

CONTENTS

Continued ...

PREFACE

Following the publication of The Health of the Nation White Paper in July 1992, the National Health Service Management Executive commissioned Handbooks on possible local approaches to each of the five Key Areas identified in the White Paper: Coronary Heart Disease and Stroke, Cancers, Mental Illness, Accidents, and HIV/AIDS and Sexual Health. The Handbooks were published in January 1993; the present document is a revision of the original Mental Illness Key Area Handbook.

The intention behind publishing the Key Area Handbooks was primarily to assist managers and directors in purchasing authorities (DHAs, FHSAs, purchasing consortia and, for mental illness, Local Authority Social Services Departments) to develop local strategies for reducing mortality and morbidity in each Key Area. A secondary aim was to disseminate widely information about local initiatives to managers and directors in provider organisations, and to group together other relevant information. It was also the Department of Health's intention that the Handbooks would be of interest to other organisations, for example those in the voluntary sector, which join together with the NHS and SSDs in alliances to improve health.

The response to the first edition of the Mental Illness Key Area Handbook has generally been very positive, and the Department has received much useful feedback. This revised edition builds on that feedback, and on policy developments which have taken place over the last year and a half. Again the approach is illustrative rather than prescriptive; managers and others will wish to use this guide selectively, according to local circumstances.

Managers and clinicians will wish to know that the Department of Health plans to publish two further documents aimed in particular at improving care for severely mentally ill people, namely, a guide to better inter-agency working, and the Mental Health Task Force's *Local Systems of Support for People with Severe Mental Health Problems – A Framework for Purchasing and Provision*.

The production of the original Key Area Handbooks was the result of a joint working venture between the Department of Health, the NHS and other organisations. The Handbooks could not have been published without the help and advice of colleagues from outside the Department. Similarly, we are very grateful for the comments and advice which we have received from a wide range of external bodies in revising the Mental Illness Key Area Handbook.

Comments on this revised edition are very welcome and should be sent to Dr Rachel Jenkins or Dr Geraldine Strathdee at the Department of Health, Wellington House, 133-155 Waterloo Road, London SE1 8UG.

ABBREVIATIONS

ASW	Approved Social Worker
CHC	Community Health Council
CMHT	Community Mental Health Team
CPA	Care Programme Approach
CPN	Community Psychiatric Nurse
DGH	District General Hospital
DH	Department of Health
DHA	District Health Authority
ECT	Electro-convulsive therapy
FHSA	Family Health Services Authority
GPFH	General Practitioner Fundholder
HEA	Health Education Authority
HAS	Health Advisory Service
IT	Information Technology
LA	Local Authority
LASS	Local Authority Social Services
LEA	Local Education Authority
MDT	Multi-disciplinary team
MRC	Medical Research Council
NHS	National Health Service
NHSME	National Health Service Management Executive
NHSE	National Health Service Executive
NSF	National Schizophrenia Fellowship
OPCS	Office of Population Censuses and Surveys
PACT	Placement, Assessment and Counselling Teams
PHCT	Primary Health Care Team
R&D	Research and Development
RDP	Research and Development for Psychiatry (now SCMH)
RCGP	Royal College of General Practitioners
RMO	Responsible Medical Officer
RSU	Regional Secure Unit
SCMH	Sainsbury Centre for Mental Health (formerly RDP)
SHA	Special Health Authority
SHSA	Special Hospitals Services Authority
SSD	Social Services Department
SSI	Social Services Inspectorate
TAPS	Team for the Assessment of Psychiatric Services

CHAPTER I

EXECUTIVE SUMMARY

EXECUTIVE SUMMARY

Introduction

1.1   The Health of the Nation identified mental illness as one of the five key areas in the Government's health strategy. The three primary targets which the White Paper set are:

- To improve significantly the health and social functioning of mentally ill people

- To reduce the overall suicide rate by at least 15% by the year 2000 (from 11.0 per 100,000 population in 1990 to no more than 9.4)

- To reduce the suicide rate of severely mentally ill people by at least 33% by the year 2000 (from the life-time estimate of 15% in 1990 to no more than 10%).

The significance of mental illness and suicide

1.2   Mental health problems are a leading cause of illness, distress, disability and mortality. For example, the all cause mortality rates for schizophrenia are estimated to be over twice that of the general population, largely due to suicide, accidents and cardio-vascular disorders. Primary care surveys have shown that at least 26% of the population consult their family doctor each year with a mental health problem. In addition, there is considerable indirect morbidity among patients' relatives and carers, who often develop psychiatric symptoms from their burden of care. Mental ill-health accounts for an estimated 14% of days lost at work (see also Appendix 1.1).

1.3   Mental illness (see Appendix 1.2 for a brief description) accounted for 18,286 recorded deaths in 1991. Within this figure, suicide is a significant cause of premature death[1]. There is now widespread evidence that suicide is preventable. Appendix 1.3 sets out important background information for managers which will put the measures outlined in this handbook to reduce suicide into context. Suicide:

- accounts for approximately 1% of all deaths annually – 5,542 deaths in 1992

- has risen by 75% in young men (aged 15-24) since 1982

- is the second most common cause of death in 15-34 year old males

- is three times higher than average in young Asian women.

1.4   Mental health problems make significant demands on the NHS, social services, employers and society generally. For example, 50% or more of all people on social

---

[1]Suicide and self inflicted injury (ICD E950-E959) and injury undetermined whether accidentally or purposely inflicted (ICD E980-E989). Coroners vary in their criteria for recording a suicide verdict. Including the category of undetermined deaths reduces the variation considerably. Most undetermined deaths are suicides.

workers' caseloads, whether generic, mental health or other specialist (eg elderly or children), have some sort of mental health problem. Suicide accounts for about 8% of all working days lost through death (ie between ages 15-64) whilst mental illness accounts for approximately 14% of NHS inpatient costs, and 91 million lost days of work a year.

1.5 These figures are likely to be underestimates because of:

- the failure of community and primary care staff to recognise some mental illness
- the failure of staff working in the acute sector to recognise psychiatric morbidity in general medical and surgical settings
- the insufficient attention given to psychological distress associated with physical diseases, particularly those associated with long-term disablement
- the substantial effect of mental illness on other morbidity and mortality statistics. For example, Standardised Mortality Ratios for people with schizophrenia are 2.5, ie two-and-a-half times the average
- the under-reporting of mental illness due to stigma.

Developing comprehensive local services

1.6 Major advances have been made in the last decade both in the understanding and management of mental illness, and of the risk factors and circumstances in which suicide occurs. Significant opportunities now exist for the effective treatment and continuing care of people with acute and severe and enduring mental illness, and the reduction of suicide rates. Developments include:

- **Changes in treatment methods** – including both psychotherapies (cognitive, behavioural, interpersonal and family therapies) and improved physical interventions (see Chapter 6)
- **Changes in treatment settings** – 31 old-style mental hospitals had been replaced by the end of 1993 out of a total of 131 in 1961 (see Chapter 6)
- **Changes in working patterns** – the development of multi-disciplinary team working, and greater involvement and influence of users and carers (see Chapter 10).

1.7 In spite of the opportunities provided by these developments, mental illness has remained a poor relation in NHS and LA management priorities. Services have been fragmented and poorly co-ordinated, resulting in poor information and inappropriately targeted resources; alliances between health and social services have not been developed to their full potential.

1.8 NHS and SSD management have a key role to play in developing and encouraging change to:

- deliver the most effective care and treatment to each individual with a mental illness

- ensure that changes in treatment and care setting take place in a systematic manner.

How to use this handbook to achieve the targets

1.9 In a situation where "need is limitless and resources finite", available resources need to be carefully targeted to ensure that they are used as cost-effectively as possible, to provide the maximum possible health and social benefits.

1.10 Due to the close co-operation required between health and social services in the delivery of the Mental Illness Key Area targets, this handbook is addressed jointly to the NHS and SSDs. It concentrates on providing practical advice to managers on the **implementation of change** necessary to achieve the targets in the mental illness key area. The handbook sets out a range of options which may be adapted to suit local circumstances. The ideas contained in the handbook are not comprehensive, but should act as stimuli for development and innovation at a local level.

1.11 Progress towards the primary targets will take time. Managers at all level of the health and social services will want to undertake an honest appraisal of the local situation and then to prioritise the action that they take. They will want to draw up a clear timescale for implementation, which fits local circumstances and needs, to help them break down the process of change into manageable stages. Managers – and practitioners – will then be able to identify milestones to set achievable but challenging targets against which progress can be monitored.

1.12 Principal themes for management action highlighted in the handbook are:

- joint-working with other agencies to promote mental health and reduce the stigma attached to mental illness (Chapters 2 and 5)

- systematic needs assessment and reviews of current service provision (Chapter 3)
- wide local consultation with all interested parties locally, in particular with users and carers, in the development of strategies and services to reduce mental illness and suicide (Chapter 4)
- the development of effective joint planning and purchasing between the NHS (including GP fundholders) and Social Services Departments (Chapters 5 and 12)
- ensuring a smooth transition from old-style institutions to community care, and full implementation of the Care Programme Approach (CPA) and care management (Chapters 6 and 9)
- facilitating and promoting staff development and multi-disciplinary working, and the development of closer working between the primary and secondary care sectors to increase the awareness, detection and treatment of mental illnesses (Chapter 10)
- the implementation of effective mental health information systems and supervision registers (Chapter 11)
- targeting a balance of prevention, treatment (including reducing dependence upon benzodiazepines), rehabilitation and continuing care effectively upon different user groups – including children and adolescents, young adults, older adults, women, people from black and other ethnic minorities, homeless people, and mentally disordered offenders
- the need for co-operative working between health, social services and criminal justice agencies to ensure that mentally disordered offenders are diverted from the criminal justice system as and when appropriate, and that they are cared for by health and social services.

The further development of primary mental health targets

1.13 The current scarcity of information on the epidemiology of mental illness and attempts to use process indicators, such as bed numbers, as proxies for outcome, have distorted service provision. We have therefore made our first target a real morbidity outcome target, for which we shall require outcome indicators. These are being developed and the target will be refined as more data becomes available.

References

ALLEBECK, P. (1989) Schizophrenia: a life-shortening disease. *Schizophrenia Bulletin* **15**, 81-89.

BEBBINGTON, P., HURRY, J., TENNANT, C., STURT, E., WING, J.K. (1981) Epidemiology of mental disorders in Camberwell. *Psychological Medicine* **11**, 561-579.

CROFT-JEFFREYS, C., WILKINSON, G. (1989) Estimated costs of neurotic disorder in UK general practice 1985. *Psychological Medicine* **19**, 549-558.

DAVIES, L., DRUMMOND, M. (1990) The economic burden of schizophrenia. *British Journal of Psychiatry* **154**, 522-525.

DEPARTMENT OF HEALTH (1991) *The Health of the Nation*. London: HMSO.

MacCARTHY, B., LESAGE, A., BREWIN C., BRUGHA T., WING, J.K. (1989) Needs for care among the relatives of long term users of day care. *Psychological Medicine* **19**, 725-736.

GOLDBERG, D.P. (1991) Filter to care—a model. In: JENKINS, R., GRIFFITHS, S. (eds) Indicators for mental health in the population. London: HMSO.

MANN, A. (1991) Public health and psychiatric morbidity. In: JENKINS, R., GRIFFITHS, S. (eds) Indicators for mental health in the population. London: HMSO.

Appendix 1.1

EPIDEMIOLOGICAL DATA ON MENTAL ILLNESS

I. The following estimates describe the disease prevalence and service contact a District/ Purchasing Consortium or Local Authority can expect amongst its resident population. The figures are based upon a population of 500,000 including 70,000 over the age of 65.

2. The disease prevalence figures below are broad estimates. As local information gathering becomes better established, the quality of this epidemiological data should improve.

Disease prevalence	
1,000–2,500	with schizophrenia – between 33 and 50% only will be in contact with mental health services
500–2,500	with affective psychosis
10,000–25,000	with depressive disorder
8,000–30,000	with anxiety states
3,500	with dementia

3. Service contact figures reflect service use rather than the need for service provision.

Service contact	
10,000	seen annually by psychiatrists
2,000–2,500	admitted to psychiatric ward annually
1,350	on CPN caseload at any time
450–500	psychiatric inpatients at any time
30,000–40,000	seen annually in general practice with diagnosed mental illness

Ordinary admissions by main diagnosis and duration of stay, NHS Hospitals, England, 1989–1990.

Main diagnosis	Total ordinary admissions	Duration of stay (days)	
		Median	Mean
Mental disorders	303,378	14	255.7
Senile & presenile organic psychotic	47,423	20	197.7
Schizophrenic psychoses	33,585	31	723.3
Affective psychoses	30,949	29	92.9
Other psychoses	33,960	15	71.7
Neurotic & personality disorders	31,382	14	49.3
Alcohol dependence syndrome	20,530	9	16.4
Drug dependence	2,967	9	18.7
Physiological malfunction from mental factors	698	2	6.6
Mental retardation	56,047	4	620.3

Source: DEPARTMENT OF HEALTH. (1993) Hospital Episode Statistics. Volume 1. Finished consultant episodes by diagnosis, operation and specialty. England: Financial year 1989-90. London: HMSO.

MENTAL ILLNESSES—BRIEF DESCRIPTIONS

Schizophrenia

involves the most basic functions that give people a feeling of individuality, uniqueness and self-direction (creating their 'reality boundary') and help them relate to others. It can cause them to hallucinate, develop feelings of bewilderment and fear, and to believe that their deepest thoughts, feelings and acts may be known to, or controlled by others.

Affective (mood) psychosis

causes profound changes in mood, either to severe depression with reduction in levels of activity, or elation with over-activity.

Depressive disorder

is where symptoms such as depressed mood, loss of interest, reduced energy, suicidal ideas, sleep and appetite disturbance exceed normal mood fluctuation.

Anxiety states

includes phobias, panic and generalised anxiety disorders where anxiety symptoms, eg worry, tension, over breathing, giddiness, cause significant distress and/or disability.

Dementia

leads to decline in intellectual functioning and memory caused by diseases of the brain, such as Alzheimer's and Vascular (blood vessel) disease.

Eating disorders

include anorexia nervosa, where severe weight loss occurs, and bulimia nervosa which both involve fear of fatness with under and over eating.

Personality disorders

involve deeply ingrained and enduring behaviour patterns, showing themselves as inflexible responses to a broad range of personal and social situations. They may be associated with distress and problems in social functioning.

Appendix 1.3

SUICIDE

"'If they want to do it, they will do it anyway' is not the case."

1. Much is known about suicide, its risk factors and the circumstances in which it occurs. A basic knowledge of the factors involved will help guide managers in ensuring that action is taken to achieve the targets.

2. Suicide is rarely a choice made unclouded by depression. Of the people who commit suicide:

> 90% have some form of mental disorder
>
> 66% have consulted their GP in the previous month
>
> 33% have expressed clear suicidal intent
>
> 25% are psychiatric outpatients.

However younger men make fewer contacts with services.

3. People who have attempted suicide in the past are at a greatly increased risk of committing suicide in the future. This risk is estimated to be approximately 100 times greater than average in the year after an attempt. Rates are also markedly increased in those recently discharged from psychiatric in-patient care.

Factors influencing suicide rates

4. The causes of suicide can be many and various, but are fundamentally the inter-action of life events, psychological state, lack of effective treatment and social support and ready access to the means to commit suicide. International comparisons, as well as variations within England between Regions, show that social and cultural factors as well as access to means influence suicide rate. Addressing all these issues will help reduce the incidence of suicide.

5. The graph on the next page shows Regional variations in suicide rates within the UK.

Death Rates* for Suicide and Undetermined Injury
by Region Persons All Ages 1989-1991

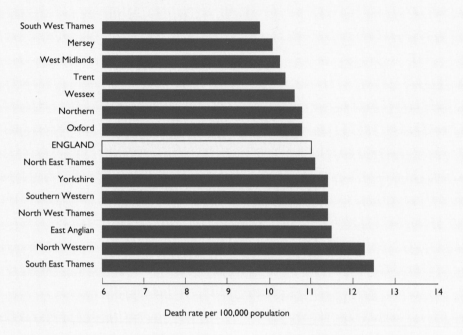

Death rate per 100,000 population

*Rates calculated using the European Standard Population

Source: Public Health Common Data Set 1992. The Health of the Nation Baseline Data (ICD E950-E959, E980-E989)

Sex and age

6. Rates of suicide are four times as high in men as in women and the difference is increasing. Although motherhood does not protect against depression, mothers of young children are less likely to commit suicide.

7. Since the early 1970s, suicide rates for men under the age of 45 have risen and are now higher than those of older men, apart from men aged 75 and over. Rates for 15-19 year olds appear to have stabilised – at more than double the rate in the early 1970s – but the rates among those aged 20-44 continue to rise. In contrast, rates for women remain lower in women aged 45 and under. The graphs on the next page highlight recent trends in suicide rates by sex and age.

Death Rates for Suicide and Undetermined Injury
by Sex and Age England

Males

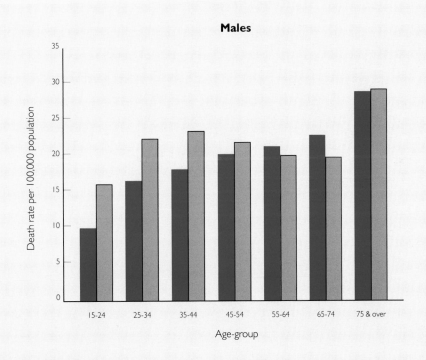

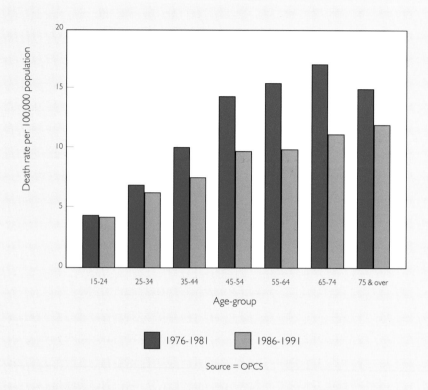

Females

Source = OPCS

Legend: 1976-1981, 1986-1991

Social Class

8. Suicide rates are highest in social class V (unskilled workers).

Employment status

9. Suicide rates are higher amongst the unemployed, although the relationship is complex. Under 10% of all those who commit suicide are unemployed at the time, although studies have shown a statistically significant link between the general male suicide rate and rises in unemployment.

Family status

10. The ending of marriages or partnerships – whether by divorce or death – has a direct impact on suicide rates. It may also have a delayed effect on children whose parents separate, leading to mental illness or suicide in later life.

Mental disorder

11. Serious mental disorder and alcohol abuse have a marked effect on lifetime suicide rates. They are estimated at:

schizophrenia	10%
affective disorder	15%
personality disorder	15%
alcohol dependence	15%

Season

12. Suicide rates are highest in the spring and early summer, notably April, May and June.

Access to means

13. The availability of easy and relatively painless methods of suicide is an important factor in influencing suicide rates.

14. The inhalation of car exhaust fumes is involved in 33% of male suicides. Tighter exhaust emission controls and the introduction of catalytic converters could have as dramatic an effect as did the reduction of the proportion of carbon monoxide in household gas in the 1960s.

15. Self-poisoning has declined with reduced prescriptions for barbiturates, but still accounts for 66% of suicides amongst women, paracetamol being commonly used.

Local suicide rates

16. Although there will be considerable variations geographically and over time for reasons outside the PHCT's control, on average the annual suicide rates shown in the following table can be expected:

Location	Suicides/annum
GP practice (list size 6,000)	1
Mental Health team (sector 50 to 100,000)	6–12 sector
	2–5 amongst patients
DHA/Purchasing consortium (500,000 population)	50–60

Measures to reduce suicide

17. Suicide rates *can* be reduced by:

- general public health measures;

- interventions by primary health care teams; and

- well-managed and responsive local health and social services, which can recognize mental illness early and make timely interventions.

Particular interventions are described in Chapter 6.

CHAPTER 2

MENTAL HEALTH PROMOTION

MENTAL HEALTH PROMOTION

Action summary

All NHS and SSD Managers

▌ Develop good practice to improve mental health in the NHS and LA workplace.

▌ Build alliances for health promotion outside the NHS and local authority social services.

▌ Co-ordinate local strategies with the Health Education Authority.

Promoting mental health and preventing mental illness

2.1 Mental illness more than many other illnesses has been the subject of immense stigma and discrimination. Health promotion can do much to improve this situation and to create a health care system which promotes the health of the nation as well as treating existing mental illness. In developing overall strategies towards Health of the Nation targets, the NHS and SSD's will want to find the appropriate local balance in resource allocation between current service provision and the Health of the Nation aspects of their work.

2.2 Unlike treatment measures which can be immediate in their effect, health promotion is a longer-term strategy. Increasing awareness about mental illness, changing public attitudes and developing strategies to prevent illness will:

- reduce the incidence of mental illness and suicide by, for example, improving coping abilities in stressful situations
- counter the fear, ignorance and stigma which still surround mental illness, and thereby help people to talk about their feelings, emotions and problems, and to seek help, without fear of being labelled or feeling a failure
- prevent the deterioration of an existing mental illness
- improve the quality of life of people with long standing, recurrent or acute mental health problems, and that of their family and friends
- maintain and improve social functioning.

Public Information Strategy for Mental Health

2.3 In March 1993, the Department of Health launched a strategy to promote mental health through a programme coordinated with major professional and voluntary groups.

2.4 An attitude survey was commissioned to provide a baseline against which to measure change. 2000 people were interviewed as part of an omnibus survey. Those interviewed were presented with a series of statements about people who have a mental illness and services provided for them. They were then asked if they agreed or disagreed with them. The statements used have their origin in similar but local studies in Toronto and the West Midlands.

2.5 Results showed that whilst stereotyping of people with mental illness is prevalent, nevertheless 92% of the population believed that we need to adopt a far more tolerant attitude towards people with mental illness; 77% agreed that mental health services should be provided through community based facilities, and 81% that the best therapy for many people with mental illness is to be part of a normal community.

However, statements about responsibility and mental illness did give cause for concern. For example, only 46% disagreed with the statement that anyone with a history of mental illness should be excluded from public office. There was also ambivalence about whether 'less emphasis should be placed on protecting the public from people with mental illness', with 39% agreeing, and 31% disagreeing.

The survey was repeated in April 1994. Analysis shows some decline in the more positive attitudes indicated above, albeit from a high baseline position.

2.6 Booklets on mental illness have been disseminated to advice centres, libraries, social service departments, employers and through GP practices:

> 'Mental Illness: What does it mean?'
>
> 'Mental Illness: Sometimes I think I can't go on anymore..'
>
> 'Mental Illness: A Guide to mental health in the workplace'
>
> 'Mental Illness: Mental health and older people'
>
> 'Mental Illness: Can children and young people have mental health problems?'
>
> 'Mental Illness: What you can do about it' (forthcoming).

2.7 A programme of activities called "Focus on Mental Health" is also being developed commencing on World Mental Health Day (10th October 1994). Contact Edith Morgan, c/o The Sainsbury Centre for Mental Health, 134-138 Borough High Street, London SE1 1LB.

NHS and SSDs direct action

2.8 The NHS and social services have a direct role in promoting mental health and preventing mental illness. Each will benefit from effective co-operation with the other in its mental health promotion work, and from networking with the voluntary sector and community groups.

2.9 Different mental health problems will be more prevalent in different parts of the local population – for example, stress related disorders in mothers with young children; living through bereavement for the elderly; coping with lack of work for unemployed people, etc. Health and social services authorities should therefore consider the priority groups for health promotion in their locality and how best to target promotional work at different age groups – children and adolescents, adults and the elderly – and at women, people from black and other ethnic minorities and lesbians and gay men. Various voluntary sector groups may have specific expertise in targeting services at these groups.

Primary prevention

2.10 Primary prevention centres on procedures to avoid the occurrence of illness or disability. A major area of direct health promotion work is the detection of at risk groups and the provision of advice and counselling. Relevant groups include:

- people without work, either through unemployment or retirement
- recently bereaved individuals
- single parents – befriending schemes for young mothers represent one approach successfully established by Homestart and Newpin
- those caring for disabled children and adults

- people who lack friends, family or other support structures
- people who are homeless or living in inadequate housing
- people suffering from sensory or physical impairment to reduce the additional risk of disabling depression
- those at risk of committing child or elder abuse

Secondary prevention

2.11 This focuses on early diagnosis and treatment to shorten episodes of illness, and to limit disability arising from illness. By preventing the knock-on consequences of mental illness for spouses, children, carers, colleagues and neighbours, secondary prevention also has a primary preventative effect. It can also reduce rates of hospitalisation and the need for costly ongoing care. Measures include:

- the early detection and effective management of depression, anxiety and cognitive impairment in primary care
- the early detection and treatment of people with psychoses
- the development of personal coping strategies to minimise the effects of conditions, for example, hearing voices.

Tertiary prevention

2.12 This focuses on measures to limit disability and handicap due to impairment or illness which is not fully curable. Measures can include:

- countering discrimination in health and social service provision against people with a history of mental illness
- providing facilities for the social and occupational rehabilitation of people with long-term mental illness
- developing coping strategies with carers and people with long-term physical or mental illness
- providing respite care for people with chronic mental illness, and support for carers.

Opportunistic advice

2.13 Health and social care professionals, particularly primary care workers, have many opportunities in their contacts with service users to identify mental illness and give advice to promote mental health. These opportunities include:

- health checks of elderly people. The diagnosis of depression in old age is often missed, yet treatment is just as effective as with younger patients
- during health visitors' contacts with children and elderly people
- in accident and emergency departments
- in social work settings.

The NHS and SSD workplace

2.14 The stresses of NHS and local authority social services work can be severe. The costs to the NHS and SSDs of mental illness can be high in terms of time off work and reduced effectiveness whilst at work. The suicide rate for doctors is twice the national average; women doctors' suicide rate is seven times the equivalent rate for other women professionals. As a major employer and participant in the Health at Work initiative, the NHS has taken on a commitment to promote the mental health of its workforce. The Department of Health has made the mental health of the NHS workforce one of the six National research priorities in mental health for the NHS Research and Development programme. The University of Sheffield has been funded to investigate workplace factors affecting mental health in 8,000 NHS staff over 4 years.

Building Alliances

2.15 Mental health promotion, particularly primary prevention, is not just a matter for health and social services departments. But the NHS and SSDs should take a lead in ensuring that mental health promotion is widely supported and integrated into different settings. Health and social agencies will want to consider how they can build alliances for mental health promotion with a variety of organisations, including:

- voluntary organisations
- the private sector

- housing departments and housing associations

- education services and schools

- youth groups

- employers and trades unions

- local media

- community and user groups.

Some suggested areas of joint working with these and other organisations are described in Chapter 5.

An Example of a Local Campaign – The Isle of Wight

2.16 The Isle of Wight Health Commission organized a Mental Health Awareness Week in April 1994, involving a healthy alliance between the Health Commission, the social services department, schools, churches, the local media and others. Particular initiatives included a tabloid insert for the local newspaper on mental illness, open days, features on local radio programmes, and special prayers to be said in local churches. For further information contact Dr Paul Bingham, Consultant in Public Health Medicine, Isle of Wight Health Commission.

References

HEALTH EDUCATION AUTHORITY (1992) Health at work in the NHS. London: Department of Health.
JENKINS, R. (1990) Towards a system of mental health outcome indicators. *British Journal of Psychiatry*, **157**, 500-514.
JENKINS, R., and CONEY, N. (1992) Preventing Mental Ill Health at Work. London: HMSO.
JENKINS, R., and WARMAN, D. (1993) Promoting Mental Health Policies in the Workplace. London: HMSO.
LAKE, B., BURGESS, J.M. (1989) Mental health and mental illness: educating sixth-formers. *British Journal of Occupational Therapy*, **52, 8,** 301-4.
MIND (1994) How to look after yourself. MIND publications.
NEWTON, J. (1992) Preventing mental illness in practice. London: Routledge & Kegan Paul.
NEWTON, J. (1988) Preventing mental illness. London: Routledge & Kegan Paul.
PARDES, H., *et al* (1989) Prevention and the field of mental health. *Annual Review of Public Health*, **10,** 403-422.
ROYAL COLLEGE OF PSYCHIATRISTS (1993) Report on Prevention and Mental Health. London: RCPsych.
TOMES, K., *et al* (1990) Health Education: effectiveness and efficiency. Chapman and Hall.
TRUTE, *et al* (1989) Social rejection of the mentally ill: a replication study of public attitude. *Social Psychiatry and Psychiatric Epidemiology*, **24,** 69-76.
WEST MIDLANDS REGIONAL HEALTH AUTHORITY (1992) The Promotion of Mental Health. Birmingham: WM Region.

CHAPTER 3

SKETCHING THE LOCAL PICTURE

SKETCHING THE LOCAL PICTURE

Action summary

DHAs (with GPFHs), FHSAs and Directors of SSDs

▌ Develop a local population profile and build up a composite picture of mental health needs.

▌ Organise information on suicide incidence.

▌ Identify local initiatives and opportunities and profile current initiatives and service provision and assess the extent to which needs are being met.

▌ Compare the suicide rates of the resident population with those of neighbouring districts, and the national rate.

Providers

▌ Use brief standardised assessment procedures of symptom state, social disability and quality of life (HoNOS scales – see Appendix 11.3).

▌ Encourage staff to co-operate with the Confidential Inquiry into Homicides and Suicides by Mentally Ill People.

Sketching the local picture

3.1 In order to meet the targets set out in the Health of the Nation, purchasers will need to develop a more detailed and coherent picture of the needs of people with mental illness locally, of local initiatives aimed at promoting mental health, and of the range of services available.

Developing a population profile

3.2 The relationship between socio-demographic characteristics and use of services, particularly admission rate, is well established. Purchasing authorities will therefore want to establish a profile of the local population. Such a profile will facilitate effective targeting of preventive activity at known high risk areas and groups. Possible relevant indicators include:

- pockets of high unemployment, particularly amongst young men

- high rates of alcohol consumption, and drug abuse

- proportion and location of people from black and other ethnic minorities, including refugees and whether established in, or new to UK
- areas of poor housing, overcrowding and lack of amenities
- numbers of homeless people
- numbers of people who are elderly and very elderly
- numbers of single parents and children in single parent families.

Additional information that could be included in drawing up a socio-demographic profile of the population is given in Appendix 3.1. OPCS census data can provide much useful local information. In addition, a number of local authorities have drawn up detailed socio-economic profiles of their populations which may be of considerable use.

3.3   It is important that GPFHs collaborate with DHAs in developing a local population profile and in needs assessment exercises. In particular, GPFHs will want to:

- obtain from the DHA/FHSA details of the population profile, local community care plans and results of needs assessment exercises for their catchment population, with particular reference to the factors identified in 3.2 above
- consider action in co-ordination with the mental health team(s) working with the practice, and the providers from whom they purchase services.

3.4   Building up an accurate picture of mental health will establish a baseline against which:

- local targets can be set
- action initiated
- progress monitored.

Local needs assessment

3.5   The use of mental health services is often more the reflection of historic circumstance, local service availability and provider priorities than a reflection of need. But health and social care needs assessment is now becoming well-established, and its application to mental illness is being developed. Assessment should take account of both health and social care needs. Methods include:

- surveys of users, carers and the local catchment population

- focus groups and depth interviews

- process information such as GP referral patterns, GP morbidity survey (currently available every 10 years), GP and IP data by diagnosis. Comparisons will also help identify training needs. In isolation, information from this source will always provide significant underestimates of actual need.

3.6 As well as establishing the general mental health needs of the population, purchasing authorities will want to identify the particular needs of different groups of service users. Needs assessment processes should be sensitive to differences of age, gender, social class and ethnicity as well as to general care needs associated with specific mental illnesses. Voluntary and community groups providing services to different sectors of the population can assist in sensitive needs assessment. Particular attention should be paid to the needs of:

People from black and other ethnic minorities

3.7 In contracting for services purchasers should take into account differences of culture and religion. In particular, purchasers should assess needs for access to:

- professionals from similar cultural backgrounds

- religious leaders

- interpreting and advocacy services

- special dietary arrangements and other culturally specific requirements.

Women

3.8 58% of mental health service in-patient admissions are women. Women's particular concerns may include:

- access to child care facilities at day centres or outpatient clinics etc

- access to respite/sitting services for women who are carers for elderly or disabled people

- the choice of a female professional, including a female keyworker

- the choice of a single sex ward (or clearly separated part of a ward)

- the availability of services for treating disorders which primarily affect women, for example eating disorders.

Mentally disordered offenders

3.9 A number of purchasers have still to give full attention, with social services and criminal justice agencies, to the needs of mentally disordered offenders. Future service development should follow the direction set by the Department of Health/Home Office review of services for mentally disordered offenders (Final Summary Report, 1992) which highlighted the importance of local, multi-agency needs assessments[1]. These should be geared in particular to assessing and meeting the need for medium and low secure services and more generally the requirements in NHS Management Executive Letter (93)54 to provide:

- an effective range of non-secure and secure services (including those for patients with special or differing needs, such as people with learning disabilities or psychopathic disorder, ethnic minorities, young people and women);
- arrangements for the multi-agency assessment and, as necessary, diversion of offenders from the criminal justice system;
- services which meet the mental health care needs of transferred or discharged prisoners;
- placements, within six months, for special hospital patients who no longer require high security.

Elderly people

3.10 Effective health and social care for elderly people with mental health problems cannot happen without:

- well-organised old age community psychiatric services for assessment and monitoring
- acute and day hospital facilities for the management of those older people with acute or enduring mental health problems
- collaboration between health and social services to provide assessment of the mental health needs of older people
- collaboration between old age psychiatry and old age medical services to provide assessment and management of:
    - the mental health needs of people presenting with physical illness, and

[1] See also NHS Management Executive Letter (93)68

> – the physical health needs of those presenting with mental illness

- adequate health service continuing and terminal care beds for people with dementia and other severe mental illnesses

- respite care

- domiciliary care

- practical advice and support for carers in dealing with, for example, behavioural problems, incontinence or immobility.

3.11 In assessing needs for services for elderly people, purchasers and providers need to remember that patients who are nominally 'elderly' may well benefit from remaining within existing service provision, rather than being transferred to specialist old age psychiatric services. Care should therefore be taken in applying any age-determined criteria for access to services.

Children and adolescents

3.12 The needs of children and adolescents are different from those of adults. Psycho-social factors which affect parents can also have distinct and separate effects on their children. In assessing needs, purchasers and providers will need to consider the child and the family, the school or college and the child's general social network.

3.13 It is essential that the services for children and adolescents are properly planned and coordinated. This is addressed in the Mini-Handbook for Child and Adolescent Mental Health, to be published later this year.

Informal Carers

3.14 Family members and other informal carers provide the majority of support for people with a severe mental illness. Following hospital closures the burden upon carers has in many cases increased. If the needs of carers are not catered for, both their health, and that of the people they care for, can suffer.

Direct services for carers would include:

- provision of information on all aspects of mental illness, in a range of formats

- access to a range of respite care facilities

– informed involvement in the planning of services, both at the global and the individual level.

Other groups

3.15 The particular needs of other groups who may have difficulty in accessing services and who may feel disenfranchised or alienated should also be identified, including:

- people who are homeless
- people suffering from both a physical and a mental illness
- people with sensory disabilities
- people with learning disabilities and mental illness – in line with HSG(92)42
- lesbians and gay men.

3.16 People with mental illness will often have needs which should be met by both health and social service providers of care. Local authorities have a statutory duty to assess the community care needs of people with a mental illness.

Wherever possible HAs and SSDs should develop joint assessment procedures, with shared forms. Such procedures should:

- ensure that individuals do not slip through the net of care
- maximise resource utilisation
- facilitate the most effective delivery of care
- reduce the number of assessments which users have to undergo.

3.17 The Department has commissioned a national psychiatric survey which is being carried out by the OPCS to establish the prevalence of mental illness. The results of this survey should be available to the service from late 1994 onwards and will provide a comparator between local needs and the national context. Details of the survey are at Appendix 3.2.

3.18 The Research Unit of the Royal College of Psychiatrists is leading work to develop appropriate instruments to assess symptom state, social disability and quality of life. These brief standardised assessment procedures will enable all patients within the mental health care system to have their health, social disability and quality of life routinely measured, enabling health outcome targets to be set and patient outcomes to be monitored both nationally and locally.

3.19 Providers should incorporate these measures and undertake regular assessments, initially on a sample basis at specified intervals. The brief standardised assessment procedures will be available to the NHS and SSDs in final form in 1995. Further information is at Appendix 11.3.

Organising information on suicides

3.20 In order to assess appropriate action to reduce suicide rates, it is necessary to develop a more comprehensive local picture of the incidence of, and factors relating to, suicide and attempted suicide.

3.21 It is also necessary to identify the number of people with a severe mental illness to measure reductions in suicide rates amongst this group. This will initially need to be collected from:

- people in contact with the social and psychiatric services
- surveys of GPs and community agencies
- hospital settings, particularly A&E departments.

3.22 DHAs and LAs will want to establish annual suicide figures. Due to the likelihood of random fluctuations at local level, health and social service authorities should consider using a five year rolling averages, using 1986-1990 data to establish an initial baseline against which changes in the local suicide rate can be measured.

3.23 Authorities will want to correlate suicide figures to a wide range of indicators – including socio-demographic background, ethnicity, age and sex (see para 3.2 and Appendix 3.1). This information should be incorporated in mental health information systems (see Chapter 11).

3.24 Suicide figures can be obtained from the OPCS, the Public Health Common Data Set and through the local coroner's office. Establishing links with pathology departments will enable access to a great deal of information about suicides contained in pathology reports. Local information on suicides should also contribute to and benefit from reports of the Confidential Inquiry into Homicides and Suicides by Mentally Ill People. Further information is at Appendix 3.3.

3.25 Multi-disciplinary review and audit in mental health services and primary care will provide valuable information about the circumstances in which people commit suicide – as well as identifying the needs of relatives and staff for support and counselling following a bereavement. Close liaison with the coroner's office will help identify cases of suicide for audit. Identifying useful information may be assisted by:

- inviting a clinician from another team to chair the audit
- inviting management to participate in relevant aspects of the mental health team audit.

Further details are given in:

Morgan H.G. 'Clinical audit of suicide and other unexpected deaths'(NHSME, 1994).

Identifying local initiatives

3.26 A local profile should help DHAs, FHSAs, and SSDs identify possible sources of help and existing initiatives aimed at promoting the mental health of the local population, including:

- health education programmes across age groups in formal and informal settings (see Chapter 5)
- media coverage of mental health issues (see Chapter 5)
- training opportunities for professionals and lay people – eg teachers, carers, youth workers (see Chapter 10)
- information on mental health and mental illness available to the general public and service users (see Chapters 4 and 13)
- job creation schemes and activities for the unemployed
- support projects for single parents
- local suicide support services
- religious organisations
- community and leisure facilities

Profiling service provision

3.27 Health and social services may have available a wide range of service settings and treatments for people with a mental illness (see Chapter 6). Sketching local service provision will assist in:

- identifying gaps in service provision and potentially redundant facilities

- evaluating different methods of service delivery

- achieving an appropriate balance between prevention, treatment, continuing care and rehabilitation

- identifying how many and what kind of staff are needed, and what their needs for support, training and education are.

3.28 Particular attention should be paid to identifying current services dedicated to the needs of:

- mentally disordered offenders in both secure and non-secure settings, including the mental health care needs of transferred or discharged prisoners

- patients in need of continuing care

- children and adolescents.

3.29 An example of a service profile for over 16s excluding services for people with dementia and mentally disordered offenders is given in Appendix 3.1. Similar service profiles can be drawn up for children, people who are elderly and mentally disordered offenders.

References

General
NHSME (1991) *Assessing health care needs. A DHA project discussion paper.* London: Department of Health.
STEVENS, A. & GABBAY,J. (1991) Needs assessment needs assessment... *Health Trends* **23**, 20-3.
Mental Health specific
BARKER, I. (Oct 1991) Purchasing for people. *Health Services Management*, 212-4.
GOLDBERG, D. & GATER, R. (1991) Estimates of need. *Psychiatric Bulletin*, **15**, 593-5.
GOLDBERG, D. & HUXLEY, P. (1992) *Common Mental Disorders. A bio-social model.* London: Routledge.
GRIFFITHS, S., WILEY, I. & JENKINS, R. [Eds] (1992) *Creating a common profile.* London: HMSO.
JARMAN, B., HIRSCH, S., WHITE, P. & DRISCOLL, R. (1992) Predicting psychiatric admission rates. *British Medical Journal,* **304**, 1146-51.
JENKINS, R. & GRIFFITHS, S. [Eds] (1991) *Indicators for mental health in the population.* London: HMSO.
THORNICROFT, G., BREWIN, C., & WING, J. (1992) *Measuring mental health needs.* London: Gaskell.
WING, J.K. (1992) *Epidemiologically-based Mental Health Needs Assessments. A Review on Psychiatric Disorders (ICD-10, F2-F6)* London: NHSME.
Black and other ethnic minorities
CONFEDERATION OF INDIAN ORGANISATIONS (1992) *A cry for change.* London: CIO.
FERNANDO, S. (1988) *Race and Culture in Psychiatry.* London: Routledge.
FERNANDO, S. (1991) *Mental Health, Race and Culture.* London: Macmillan.
FRANCIS, E., *et al.* (1989) Black people and psychiatry in the UK: an alternative to institutional care. *Psychiatric Bulletin,* **13**, 482-5.
LOWE, F. (27 August 1992) Cut off from care. *Community Care.*
MIND (1994) MIND'S Policy on Black and minority ethnic people and mental health
MOODLEY, P. (1987) The Fanon Project: a day centre in Brixton. *Bulletin of the Royal College of Psychiatrists,* **11**, 417-418.
MOODLEY, P. (1990) Blacks and Psychiatry: a framework for understanding access to psychiatric services. *Psychiatric Bulletin,* **14**, 538-40.
Women
MIND. (1992) *Policy on women and mental health.* London: MIND Publications.
MIND (1994) *Eve fights back.* London: MIND Publications.

WOMEN AND MENTAL HEALTH INTERNATIONAL CONFERENCE COMMITTEE (1991) Women and Mental Health. *British Journal of Psychiatry*. **158 (supplement 10).**

Children and Adolescents

QUINTON, D. & RUTTER, M. (1984) Parents with children in care. *Psychology and Psychiatry,* **25**, 211-229.

Mentally Disordered Offenders

NHS MANAGEMENT EXECUTIVE (1992) *Executive Letters (92)6 and (92)24.*

JONES, D. & DEAN, N. (1992) Assessment of need for services for mentally disordered offenders and patients with similar needs. *Health Trends,* **24**, 48.

DEPARTMENT OF HEALTH/HOME OFFICE (1992) *Review of health and social services for mentally disordered offenders and others requiring similar services: Final Summary Report (Cm 2088).* London: HMSO.

Homicides

CONFIDENTIAL INQUIRY INTO HOMICIDES AND SUICIDES BY MENTALLY ILL PEOPLE (1994) A preliminary report on homicide. London: Confidential Inquiry.

Suicides

MORGAN, H.G. Clinical audit of suicide and other unexpected deaths (NHSME, 1994).

CHARLTON, J., *et al.* (1992) Trends in suicide deaths in England and Wales. *Population Trends,* **69**, 10-16.

CHARLTON, J., *et al.* (1993) Suicide deaths in England and Wales – Trends in factors associated with suicide deaths. *Population Trends,* **71**, 34-42.

GARDNER, R. (1989) Guidelines on the clinical management of suicidal patients in psychiatric units. *Psychiatric Bulletin,* **13** 561-564.

HEALTH ADVISORY SERVICE (1994) Suicide prevention: the challenge confronted. London: HMSO.

JENKINS, R., *et al.* (1994) The Prevention of Suicide. London: HMSO. Further references are on p.79.

Appendix 3.1

ASSESSING SERVICE NEED AND PROVISION

Establishing a Socio-Demographic Profile

1. The following outlines information that can be used in drawing up a socio-demographic profile. It will need to be supplemented by other population groups of local relevance, for example refugees:

POPULATION BY AGE GROUP:

    0-14 years

    (15-17 years)

    15-64 years

    65-79 years

    80 and above

      Total

SOCIAL CLASS

    A-E

UNEMPLOYMENT RATES:

    Correlated to:

    age

    ethnicity

    sex

JARMAN INDEX

POPULATION DENSITY:

    Urban

    Semi-rural

    Rural

ETHNIC GROUPS:

    White – UK born

    White – Irish

    White – Other

    Black – Caribbean

    Black – African

    Black – other

    Indian

    Pakistani

    Bangladeshi

    Chinese

    Other

    Total

HOMELESSNESS:

    Homeless – bed and breakfast

    Homeless – sleeping rough

    Homeless – other

CHILDREN:

    Number looked after by Social Services Dept

Establishing current services

2. The following table gives an example of some of the information that may be useful in drawing up a profile of current services.

Residential Accommodation	Places/ 100,000 popn.	Day Care	No. places	
Current availability: Special hospital[1] Medium Secure: NHS Private Local secure units				Court diversion scheme Available: Y/N
Acute unit: In mental hospital In general hospital In other location		Day hospital: In-patients Out-patients		Sufficient staff to allow for special (1:1) observation policies on acute wards when required Y/N
24 hours NHS accommodation		Day care: rehabilitation/ continuing support	NHS LA Vol	Sector teams – including intensive domiciliary support capability Available Y/N
Mental nursing homes		Employment schemes: Dept. Employment Other NHS/ LASS/ Vol		No. of care managers (wte)
Residential care homes		Support groups/ drop-in centres		
Unstaffed group homes				No. of GP counsellors
Adult placement scheme				No. of GP practice-based clinics/week

[1]ie number/100,000 population of District residents currently in such accommodation.

NATIONAL SURVEY OF PSYCHIATRIC MORBIDITY

1. The Department of Health has commissioned a national survey of psychiatric morbidity. This will supplement local needs assessment surveys and will provide information to DHAs and SSDs to assist in needs assessment exercises.

2. The aims of the national survey are:

   - to estimate the prevalence of psychiatric morbidity according to diagnostic category among adults in England
   - to identify the nature and extent of social disabilities as a result of mental illness
   - to examine the varying use of services and the receipt of care in relation to mental illness and the resulting social disabilities
   - to investigate the risk factors which are associated with mental illness.

3. The survey seeks to cover all sectors of the population by including adults living in communal establishments – hospitals, homes and hostels – as well as those with housing needs and those living in private households. It is being carried out in three stages:

   - a screening questionnaire
   - a diagnostic schedule
   - a questionnaire covering services, care, social disabilities and risk factors.

4. The results of the national survey will be available to the NHS and SSDs from late 1994 to supplement local needs assessment processes.

Appendix 3.3

CONFIDENTIAL INQUIRY INTO HOMICIDES AND SUICIDES BY MENTALLY ILL PEOPLE

1. The Department of Health has established a Confidential Inquiry into Homicides and Suicides by Mentally Ill People. The Inquiry aims to discover avoidable causes of death and to determine best clinical practice, by means of detailed examinations of the circumstances surrounding such events. A multi-disciplinary Steering Committee, including management, nursing, psychiatric and social work representation, has been formed. The inquiry is being led by the Royal College of Psychiatrists supported by other relevant professional organisations.

2. When a suicide or homicide by a mentally ill person in contact with the specialist services is identified:

    - health and social care professionals involved in the care or treatment of the deceased, or the perpetrator, are sent a questionnaire
    - information is collected from professional staff on a confidential and **voluntary** basis, collated and anonymised
    - the information will be examined so as to draw lessons from the specific and cumulative events.

3. A pilot collection of data commenced in July 1992 to investigate events occurring on the rare occasions where a homicide is committed by a mentally ill person.

4. The inquiry was extended in June 1993 to include suicides of people in contact with or recently discharged from psychiatric care.

5. The preliminary report on homicides was published in August 1994.

Contact: Unit Office: PO Box 1515, LONDON SW1X 8PL

Tel/Answerphone: 071 823 1031
Fax: 071 823 1035

CHAPTER 4

SEEKING LOCAL VIEWS

SEEKING LOCAL VIEWS

Action summary

DHAs (with GPFHs), FHSAs, SSDs and service providers

▌ Consult all interested parties locally on needs assessment and service delivery on an ongoing basis.

▌ Provide practical support for user involvement in consultation exercises, including provision of resources where appropriate, and support for the work of independent advocacy services.

▌ Maximise user and carer involvement in developing health and social care plans.

Seeking local views

4.1 Effective local consultation by purchasers is a vital element in the needs assessment process. Both purchasers and providers will also benefit from consulting users of services to inform the qualitative aspects of service provision. By ensuring that the most appropriate services are being delivered, health and social outcomes will be improved and the Health of the Nation targets more easily met.

4.2 Purchasers and providers will each want to seek local opinion for their particular interests. Local consultation will provide important information on, amongst other things:

- local views and preferences about the range of services and treatments available, and the method of delivery (for example, on issues such as mixed wards or the choice of a key worker)
- access to services
- information about services
- the quality and appropriateness of care.

Whom to consult

4.3 Both purchasers and providers should consult as widely as possible:

- Service users – especially women and people from black and other ethnic minorities, both individually and through user groups and Patient Councils
- Patient advocates
- National and local voluntary sector eg MIND, NSF, MHF, CRUSE, Samaritans, Council of Voluntary Services
- Community Health Councils
- Carers – individually, and through carer groups
- Health and social service professionals – especially GPs and other primary health care team members, psychiatrists, community mental health nurses, and social workers
- Housing, education and police authorities
- Duty and local magistrates and solicitors.

4.4 For consultation to be meaningful, without arousing unrealistic expectations, purchasers and providers need to:

- give those consulted adequate time to give a constructive response
- indicate how far their comments are likely to influence policy.

Involving service users

4.5 Involving service users is particularly important in mental health services. Users will not only have views about the food on a ward, but also about the quality and appropriateness of care they are receiving either in a hospital, residential home or the community. Users and carers have, for example, consistently expressed preferences for community-based services. User groups can be a powerful means of enabling users to develop the confidence to express their views and make best use of services .

4.6 LAs have a duty to consult fully with users and their carers in drawing up and monitoring community care plans. NHS purchasers and providers, including GPs, have a similar responsibility.

4.7 Involving users with the most severe mental illnesses and the most long-standing health and social problems may pose particular problems. However, involving them in the planning and provision of services will help increase their self-esteem, and is central to the creation of appropriate and responsive services.

4.8 Asking people for their opinions will raise expectations that those views will be acted upon. This may not always be possible, for example because of financial constraints or because conflicting viewpoints are offered (perhaps between service users and carers). A clear explanation of the constraints on action should therefore be given when people's views are sought.

4.9 Effective consultation involves:

- providing full information in an easily accessible form
- using a wide range of techniques to facilitate participation – for example, surveys, focus groups, depth interviews and speaking to user-only groups
- listening to the views of local people and involving them in discussions and the decision making process
- acting upon views
- reporting back to those who were consulted, explaining how decisions were reached.

4.10 Practical assistance will often need to be offered to service users and carers to facilitate their involvement, for example by:

- paying expenses for travel and administration etc
- ensuring that an independent advocate is available
- making information available in appropriate languages, with interpreters for people whose main language is not English, or who have sensory impairments
- facilitating the development of user-led groups.

Involving users in their own health and social care
Information

4.11 Providers need to empower service users to play as full a part as possible in their own health and social care. An essential building block is ensuring that information is made available as a matter of course to service users. This will include appropriate information on:

- rights – including welfare rights and those set out in the Patient's Charter
- services – including access, and quality standards
- treatments, medication (including side effects) and coping strategies
- complaints and redress procedures
- the Mental Health Act 1983 (where appropriate)
- self-help groups and community networks.

4.12 Providers will need to ensure that information is:

- available at the time and place of need
- appropriate
- accessible – using an appropriate level of language
- available in different media – written, oral and visual.

Supporting advocacy services

4.13 Managers will need to consider the most appropriate mechanisms for enabling users to utilise that information to define their treatment in consultation with the specialists involved in their care. One particular method is by establishing advocacy services.

4.14 Advocacy is about giving the individual user a voice and getting the NHS and SSDs to listen to that voice and take account of users' needs and preferences. In order to ensure that there is no conflict of interest in the representation of users' views, advocacy therefore needs to be independent of service provision.

4.15 Purchasers can support advocacy projects by:

- commissioning the provision of independent advocacy by a third party within the service provider setting
- incorporating appropriate clauses within the contract with the provider unit to guarantee the advocate a voice.

4.16 Purchasers and providers can additionally support advocacy projects by establishing mechanisms whereby the advocate can influence the decision making process – through, for example, a Steering Group and direct access to senior management. The

United Kingdom Advocacy Network, in collaboration with the Mental Health Task Force, has drawn up a draft Code of Practice for Advocacy and is consulting on it. A final version will be widely available by the end of 1994.

Resources

Regional Health Information Services.
National Disability Information Project, Policy Studies Institute, 100 Park Village East, London NW1 3SR. Tel: 071 387 2171

References

General

NHSME (January 1992). *Local voices: the views of local people in purchasing for health. EL(92)1* London: NHSME.
SHROPSHIRE HEALTH AUTHORITY (1992) *Getting to the Core: A practical guide to understanding users' experience in the health service.* Shropshire Health Authority in conjunction with University of Birmingham.

Mental health specific

BARKER, I. & PECK, E. [Eds] (1987) *Power in strange places: user empowerment in mental health services.* Good Practices in Mental Health.
BASSETT, T. *et al* (1988) *Involving service users in community mental health services.* In the GPMH and IAMHW information pack Community Mental Health Teams/Centres. Good Practices in Mental Health.
BEEFORTH, M., CONLAN. E., FIELD, V., HOSAER, B. & SAYCE, L. (1990) *Whose service is it anyway? Users' views on coordinating community care.* Research and Development for Psychiatry, 134-138 Borough High Street, London SE1 1LB.
GOOD PRACTICES IN MENTAL HEALTH (1990) *Advocacy information pack.* Good Practices in Mental Health, 380-384 Harrow Road, London W9 2HU.
JOWELL, T. & RITCHIE, J. (1988) Listening to their needs. *Social Work Today,* **19,38,** 18.
LINDOW, V. (1991) Towards user power. *Health Service Journal,* **101, 5266,** 18.
MCIVER, S. (1991) *Obtaining the views of users of mental heath services.* London: King's Fund Centre.
MENTAL HEALTH MEDIA COUNCIL (1992) *From Anger to Action.* Video.
MIND (1991) *User involvement policy.* London: MIND.
MIND (1992) *The MIND guide to advocacy in mental health.* MIND.
NSF (1992) *How to involve users and carers.* London.
READ, J. & WALLCRAFT, J. (1992) *Guidelines for empowering users of mental health services.* London: COHSE/MIND.
READ, J. & WALLCRAFT, J. (1994) *Guidelines on advocacy for mental health workers.* MIND/UNISON.
SMITH, H. (1988) *Collaboration for change: partnership between service users, planners and managers of mental health services.* London: King's Fund Centre.
TOOK, M. & EVANS, T. (1990) *Provision of community services for mentally ill people and their carers: a survey for the Department of Health into the view of the NSF on community services.* London: National Schizophrenia Fellowship.

Information for users and carers

GRIMSHAW, C. (1992) *A-Z of Welfare Benefits for People with a Mental Illness.* London: MIND.
DEPARTMENT OF HEALTH (1993) *Mental Illness: What does it mean?; Mental Illness: Sometimes I think I can't go on anymore..; Mental Illness: A Guide to Mental Health in the workplace;* (1994) *Mental Illness: can children and young people have mental health problems?; Mental Illness: Mental Health and older people.* (All these booklets can be obtained by writing to BAPs, Health Publications Unit, Heywood Stores, Manchester Road, Heywood, Lancs. OL10 2PZ.)
MENTAL HEALTH FOUNDATION *Schizophrenia and the family.*
MIND *Understanding – mental illness; bereavement; caring; talking treatments; phobias & obsessions; anxiety.*
NSF. *Schizophrenia.*
ROYAL COLLEGE OF PSYCHIATRISTS. *Depression; Anxiety and Phobias; Anorexia and Bulimia; Bereavement; Surviving Adolescence; Sleep Problems; Fact sheets.*
SANE. *Schizophrenia; Anxiety, phobias & obsessions; Depressive illness.*

CHAPTER 5

DEVELOPING LOCAL ALLIANCES

DEVELOPING LOCAL ALLIANCES

Action Summary

All NHS and SSD Managers

■ Develop better co-operative working between primary and secondary health care and between health and social services.

■ Develop alliances with a wide range of other local and national organisations to develop mental health initiatives.

The need for alliances

5.1 The Health of the Nation targets for mental illness cannot be achieved by the NHS and SSDs alone. Collaborative approaches, involving the whole range of relevant agencies, provide the most effective way forward to alleviate mental illness and reduce suicide.

5.2 Building alliances will take time, effort and understanding. The benefits should include:

● a more comprehensive picture of local health needs, which can be shared widely

● other agencies setting their own targets for mental health

● co-ordinating action to maximise the effective use of resources

● a better understanding of mental illness, and the ways in which social factors, and alcohol and drug abuse, contribute to mental illness and suicide rates

● a better range of services for mentally disordered offenders, helping to avoid unnecessary imprisonment with the consequent risk of suicide or self-harm.

Key alliances

Primary and secondary care

5.3 People suffering from a mental illness will only receive coordinated care and treatment if primary and secondary care services are well-integrated. As community services are developed, the need for greater co-operative working increases. FHSAs and DHAs should consider ways of greater integration of care through:

● involving FHSAs, GPFHs and other primary care providers in the development of DHA purchasing plans, and in joint purchasing arrangements with SSDs

- joint training of staff and increased team working
- developing joint mental health promotion initiatives
- developing locality-based commissioning focused on local authority wards
- supporting the development of guidelines and protocols.

5.4 Locality based commissioning, or sectorisation – which makes a mental health team responsible for a geographically defined population of between 50 and 100,000 – has developed rapidly in the NHS with 80% of DHAs sectorising their services. Effective management is necessary if locality-based commissioning is to work in the best interests of the service user. Purchasers should ensure that:

- a choice of consultant or other mental health worker (eg female or male) is available within sectors
- referral to secondary care services and social workers across sector boundaries is unrestricted if a GP considers that referral outside the local sector is necessary, for example to access specialist skills
- closer working relationships between primary care and secondary care or community services are effectively developed, reducing the potential for severely mentally ill people to fall through the net of care

5.5 From April 1993, all GP Fundholders became responsible for purchasing community mental health services for their patients, in addition to their current responsibilities for outpatient mental health services. DHAs, SSDs and GPFHs need to liaise closely over needs assessment, purchasing and service planning.

NHS and Local Authority Social Services Departments

5.6 Although the line between health and social care for people with mental illness is difficult to draw, health and SSDs at local level must agree means of identifying which needs of individual patients are properly the responsibility of which agency. The implementation of Care Management and the Care Programme Approach (see Chapter 9) make effective co-operation a prerequisite to the effective delivery of care to people with mental illness.

5.7 The Mental Illness Specific Grant has greatly improved joint planning between health and social services. Joint planning and working can help at all points of service provision, including:

- needs assessment
- purchasing
- service delivery
- monitoring and evaluation.

5.8 LASSDs currently obtain Special Transitional Grant (STG) to purchase community care services. Health staff should seek to liaise closely with social services colleagues to ensure that mentally ill people benefit from the STG.

Voluntary sector organisations

5.9 The voluntary sector is a source of considerable expertise, and can offer opportunities for statutory agencies to engage with people suffering from mental illness who otherwise do not access their services. In its independent role, the voluntary sector acts both to monitor policy and provision and as a catalyst to change. This independence of view should be protected in any contractual arrangements between the NHS/SSDs and the voluntary sector.

5.10 The voluntary sector can be effective in:

- working to de-stigmatise social attitudes towards mental illness
- monitoring services and evaluating their effectiveness
- providing specialised advice to reduce and counter social stress, eg Citizen's Advice Bureaux, Family Welfare Associations
- helping in the provision of a range of comprehensive local services.

5.11 Support for voluntary organisations which have access to people at high risk of depression and suicide can be particularly important. Self-help groups can also be especially helpful in providing support for individuals with mental illness, and their families.

5.12 The precariousness of much voluntary sector funding should be recognised. The NHS/SSDs can provide direct financial support for projects and administration and should seek to ensure that the likely level of funding is indicated well in advance. In addition, managers can:

- involve voluntary organisations in their advisory framework
- make available resources such as the use of premises for meetings, other facilities and management support.

5.13 In addition to local branches of national organisations, unaffiliated groups may exist in your area. The National Council for Voluntary Organisations should hold addresses and contacts for these. A list of national voluntary organisations in mental health is at Appendix 5.1.

Independent mental health sector

5.14 The independent sector offers a wide range of mental health services, including specialist services, intensive secure units, long term psychiatric services, behavioural treatment and substance abuse treatment.

The independent sector can be effective in:

- offering a range of mental health services which complement those offered by the NHS and provide choice for mental health users
- facilitating the development of innovative services
- meeting needs for assessment and care of more challenging and potentially dangerous patients.

Other major alliances

Local authorities

5.15 Local authorities can have a powerful influence on mental health. In addition to the mental health services provided by social services departments, and SSDs' potential involvement in education and housing discussed below, local authorities can promote mental health by ensuring that:

- accessible and affordable recreational facilities are available for their residents

- children have safe environments in which to play

- physical, emotional and sexual abuse in children is detected as early as possible

- community facilities are available for unemployed people, women at home, older people, people with chronic sickness, etc.

5.16 Many suicides also occur on property under local authority jurisdiction. Joint working may lead to initiatives to reduce suicides at these points – for example, with fencing off or using safety-netting at high points such as cliffs and bridges and locating telephone boxes displaying helpline numbers at high risk spots.

Education and youth services

5.17 Effective collaboration between health, education and social services is essential to achieve the assessment, provision and treatment required to meet the needs of children and adolescents. There are opportunities for mental health promotion in schools within formal educational as well as informal youth settings. The NHS and SSDs can liaise with LEAs, churches, government bodies, schools, and head teachers and governors in public and private education to develop health promotion within the school curriculum, and to identify complementary activity outside the school, for example in youth clubs and community groups.

The housing sector

5.18 The success of community care for mentally ill people depends crucially on the provision of a variety of accommodation. It is vital that health authorities and social services make alliances with the housing sector – particularly local authority housing departments and local housing associations. This can help ensure that, for example:

- health and social services interests are represented in the Local Authority Housing Investment Programme (HIP)

- people with mental illness are fairly represented in the housing special needs quota

- rapid response is made by mental health teams to requests for assistance where complaints or difficulties arise in relation to people who are thought, or known to have mental health problems

- cluster flat schemes are developed where a small number of patients live together

- warden-assisted accommodation for people with mental illness becomes more common

- the number of people, particularly those with mental illness, living in bed and breakfast accommodation, direct access hostels or on the streets is reduced

- the threat of eviction, which costs housing organisations time and trouble, is alleviated. Evicted residents can be lost to mental health services.

5.19 Health authorities and LASSDs should also encourage housing departments to employ resettlement officers to help mentally ill people resettle in the community if they do not already do so, and to employ people in Homeless Persons Units able to identify clients with mental health needs.

Criminal justice system

5.20 Alliances at both purchaser and provider level between health and social services can be developed with:

- police services
- probation services
- prison services
- Courts
- The Crown Prosecution Service
- duty solicitors and local Law Societies
- local law centres
- voluntary agencies working with mentally disordered offenders.

5.21 Such alliances will contribute to:

- a better understanding by criminal justice officials of the Mental Health Act 1983 and the needs of mentally disordered offenders. This should lead to a greater willingness to call upon psychiatric and social work personnel for assessments

- the efficient development of court and pre-trial diversion schemes, and the transfer of mentally disordered offenders to community support or hospitals

- the development of links between area (Woolf) committees for the criminal justice system and health and social services.

5.22 Each prison establishment has a Suicide Prevention Management Group, which is responsible for reviewing incidents, maintaining staff awareness, ensuring good communication between staff and outside agencies and developing local prevention policy.

Employers and trades unions

5.23 The workplace can be a major cause of stress affecting mental health, smoking and alcohol consumption as well as work performance. Over ninety million days sick leave – amounting to four days for each worker – are certified as due to mental illness each year. This figure understates time off from work due to mental ill health because it takes no account of absence wrongly attributed to physical illness, or of uncertified absence. Mental ill health also leads to reduced work performance, including poor decision making, and higher turnover of staff, resulting in the loss of valuable experience and skills. The issue affects all employers. Health Promotion Departments can work with local employers and workers to develop strategies for mental health in the workplace.

5.24 The reports of the Department of Health and Confederation of British Industry-sponsored conferences on mental health set out examples of good practice. As part of its Public Information Strategy, the Department of Health has also produced "A Guide to Mental Health in the Workplace" about workplace mental health policies.

5.25 The Department of Health has formed a broadly based working committee to advise on good practice in the workplace. The committee includes representatives from the Health and Safety Executive, the Confederation of British Industries, the Trades Union Congress, the Advisory, Conciliation and Arbitration Service, and the Health Education Authority.

5.26 Some DHAs currently offer occupational mental health services within employment settings. DHAs will wish to develop and expand the availability of these schemes, working closely with employers to ensure appropriate targeting of such services and the most effective use of NHS expertise.

Employment services

5.27 Enabling people with mental illness to return to work or find employment for the first time is a key part of their rehabilitation. Local Placement, Assessment and Counselling Teams, run by the employment services and accessed through job centres, provide a route to Ability Development Centres. These centres, which are replacing traditional Employment Rehabilitation Centres, can give expert advice.

Local media

5.28 The NHS and SSDs can collaborate with the media to improve understanding of mental health issues through the encouragement of:

- non-stigmatising reporting of mental health issues in press, radio and TV
- the inclusion of a regular health column in local press where this does not already exist, and the specific inclusion of mental health issues
- radio counselling programmes
- publicity for independent help and advice, including children's advice centres.

5.29 Health Promotion Departments can also take paid advertising space where appropriate.

References
Education
NATIONAL CURRICULUM COUNCIL (1990) *Curriculum Guidance 5.* London: Department of Education.
WHO/COUNCIL OF EUROPE/COMMISSION OF THE EUROPEAN COMMUNITIES (May 1993) The European Network of Health-promoting Schools.
HOPSON, B. AND SCALLY, M. (1988) Lifeskills Teaching Programmes. Leeds: Lifeskills Publishing.
Primary Care
BENNETT, C. (1989) General Practitioner assessment of the Worcester Development Project. *Journal of the Royal College of General Practitioners,* **39**, 106-9.
JENKINS, R., FIELD, V., & YOUNG, R [Eds] (1992) *The primary care of schizophrenia.* London: HMSO.
JENKINS, R., NEWTON, J. & YOUNG, R. [Eds] (1992) *Prevention of depression and anxiety in General Practice: the role of the primary care team.* London: HMSO.
JENKINS, R. (1992) Forward Look: Developments in Primary Care of Mental Health. *International Review of Psychiatry,* **4**, 237-242.
KENDRICK, T. (1994) Fund-holding and commissioning general practitioners. Recent government policy and legislation. *Psychiatric Bulletin,* **18, 4**, 196-199.
NATIONAL HEALTH SERVICE MANAGEMENT EXECUTIVE (1992) *Guidance on the extension of the hospital and community health services elements of the GP Fundholding scheme from 1 April 1993.* (EL(92)48). Health Care Directorate (Service Development). Leeds: NHSME.
Housing departments
SONE, K. (8 June 1992) Raise the roof. *Community Care* 14-15.
Criminal Justice System
CASSIDY, J. (1994) Joining forces. *Nursing Times* **90, 2**, 16-17.
HOME OFFICE (1990). *Provision for mentally disordered offenders.* (Circular 66/90). London: Home Office.
JAMES, D.V. & HAMILTON, L.W. (1991) The Clerkenwell scheme. Assessing efficacy and cost of a psychiatric liaison service to a magistrates court. *British Medical Journal,* **303**, 282-285.
JONES, D. & DEAN, N. (1992) Assessment of need for services for mentally disordered offenders and patients with similar needs. *Health Trends,* **24**, 48.
JOSEPH, P.L. & POTTER, M. (1990) Mentally disordered homeless offenders – diversion from custody. *Health Trends,* **22, 2**, 51-3.

Employment

DEPARTMENT OF HEALTH (1993) A Guide to Mental Health in the Workplace. Heywood: DH.
HEALTH EDUCATION AUTHORITY (1992) *Health at work in the NHS*. London: DH.
JEE, M. & REASON, L. (1988) *Action on Stress at Work*. London: Health Education Authority.
JENKINS, R. & CONEY, N. [Eds.] (1992) *Prevention of ill health at work*. London: HMSO.
JENKINS, R. & WARMAN, D. [Eds.] (1992) *Promoting mental health policies in the workplace*. London: HMSO.
MENTAL HEALTH MEDIA COUNCIL (1992). *Working Life: an employers guide to mental health issues and recruitment*. Video.
MIND (1992) *Action Pack on Employment and Mental Health*. London: MIND.
MENTAL HEALTH TASK FORCE (1993) *Meeting need. Leisure and Unemployment*. Video.
MENTAL HEALTH TASK FORCE (1994) *Meeting need. Supported accommodation*. Video.
STUART M. (1990) *MIND Guide to Employment Projects*. London: MIND.

NATIONAL VOLUNTARY ORGANISATIONS

Afro-Caribbean Mental Health Association.

35-37 Electric Avenue, London SW9 8JP [071 737 3603]

Alzheimer's Disease Society.

Gordon House, 10 Greencoat Place, London SW1P 1PH [071 306 0606]

Association for Post-Natal Illness.

25 Jerdan Place, London SW6 1BE [071 386 0868]

CRUSE – Bereavement Care.

Cruse House, 126 Sheen Road, Richmond, Surrey TW9 1UR [081 940 4818]

Depressives Anonymous.

36 Chestnut Avenue, Beverley, Humberside HU17 9QU [0482 860619]

Eating Disorders Association.

Sackville Place, 44 Magdalen Street, Norwich NR3 1JE [0603 621414].

Good Practices in Mental Health.

380-384 Harrow Road, London W9 2HU [071 289 2034/3060]

Guidepost Trust.

Two Rivers, Station Lane, Witney, OXON OX8 6BH [0993 772886] (Provides supported housing).

Homestart.

2 Salisbury Road, Leicester LE1 7QR [0533 554988]

Making Space.

46 Allen Street, Warrington, Cheshire WA2 7JB [0925 571680] (Serves mainly Yorkshire and the North West of England.)

Manic Depression Fellowship.

8-10 High Street, Kingston-Upon-Thames KT1 1EY [081 974 6550]

Mental After-Care Association.

25 Bedford Square, London WC1B 3HW [071 436 6194]

Mental Health Foundation.

37 Mortimer Street, London W1N 7RJ [071 580 0145]

MIND.

Granta House, 15–19 Broadway, Stratford, LONDON E15 4BQ [081 519 2122]

NEWPIN.

Sutherland House, 35 Sutherland Square, LONDON SE1 3EE [071 703 6236]

National Black Mental Health Association.

Macro House, 182 Soho Hill, Handsworth, Birmingham, B19 1AF

National Schizophrenia Fellowship.

28 Castle Street, Kingston upon Thames, Surrey KT1 1SS [081 547 3937]

Phobic Action.

Hornbeam House, Claybury Grounds, Manor Road, Woodford Green, Essex IG8 8PR [081 559 2551]

RELATE.

Herbert Grey College, Little Church St, Rugby CV21 3AP [0788 573241]

Richmond Fellowship for Community Mental Health.

8 Addison Road, Kensington, London W14 8DL [071 603 6373]

SANE.

2nd Floor, 199–205 Old Marylebone Road, London NW1 5QD [071 724 6520]

Samaritans.

10 The Grove, Slough SL1 1QP [0753 532713]

SERVOL Community Trust.

227–235 Dudley Road, Winson Green, Birmingham B18 4EJ [021 454 3081]

Survivors Speak Out.

33 Lichfield Road, Cricklewood, London NW2

The Sainsbury Centre for Mental Health (formerly RDP)

134–138 Borough High Street, London SE1 1LB [071 403 8790]

Turning Point.

101 Backchurch Lane, London E1 1LU [071 702 2300)

United Kingdom Advocacy Network.

Premier House, 14 Cross Burgess Street, Sheffield S1 2HG [0742 753131]

Young Minds

22A Boston Place, London NW1 6ER [071 724 7262].

The National Council of Voluntary Organisations.

Regent's Wharf, 8 All Saints Street, London N7 9RL [071 713 6161] (can provide information about local activity)

CHAPTER 6

IDENTIFYING AND ASSESSING AVAILABLE INTERVENTIONS

IDENTIFYING AND ASSESSING AVAILABLE INTERVENTIONS

<blockquote>

Action summary

NHS Purchasers and Directors of SSDs

▮ Identify the range of service delivery options.

▮ Assess the appropriateness of different service options to the needs of the resident population.

NHS providers

▮ Ensure the provision of appropriate service interventions in mental health and general medical and surgical settings.

</blockquote>

Options in mental health care

6.1 A wide range of interventions is theoretically available for the care, treatment and rehabilitation of people with mental illness. Much research has been carried out nationally on their effectiveness for particular service user groups. However, the variable levels of care provision around the country suggest that many managers and professionals may be unaware of the options available, or their particular value in different conditions. Examples include the use of cognitive and interpersonal therapies in the treatment of depression and eating disorders; and family therapy and early intervention in treatment of schizophrenia.

6.2 Purchasers will need to identify the range of possible interventions to ensure that purchasing plans are fully developed to meet assessed needs. They will also want to review research and to supplement it with local analysis so as to achieve the most cost-effective delivery of care to meet assessed needs within their District.

6.3 Purchasers will want to ensure that they identify appropriate services to meet the needs of particular groups of service users (see Chapter 3). For example, the high levels of psychiatric morbidity in homeless people, and their difficulties in accessing services, may require specific initiatives such as the Inner London Homeless Mentally Ill Initiative and the work of the Nottingham Hostels Liaison Group.

6.4 This chapter sets out some basic information for managers on the available options to enable them to develop a local range of comprehensive services and treatments. It covers:

- different service settings
- different treatment methods
- specific interventions to reduce suicide.

Service settings

6.5 Care outside the institutionalised setting of large mental hospitals can improve health outcomes. Studies in Nottingham and in the USA over a 10–15 year period demonstrate that establishing rehabilitation services with a range of community-based residential and day care facilities, and mental health teams, can lead to good outcomes in schizophrenic patients who previously would have been institutionalised.

6.6 It is imperative to put in place a comprehensive range of day, residential and domiciliary services before a large mental hospital is closed to ensure appropriate replacement facilities are available for discharged patients, and for new patients coming into the care of the specialist services.

6.7 Comprehensive purchasing guidance in relation to children and adolescents is contained in the Department's recently published Mini-Handbook on Child and Adolescent Mental Health to be published later this year.

6.8 The following table sets out a range of service settings for adults.

	Acute/emergency care	Rehabilitation/continuing care
Home-based	Intensive home support Emergency duty teams Sector teams	Domiciliary services Key workers Care management
Day care	Day hospitals	Drop-in centres Support groups Employment schemes Day care
Residential support	Crisis accommodation Acute units Local secure units	Ordinary housing Unstaffed group homes Adult placement schemes, hospital hostels Residential care homes Mental nursing homes 24 hour NHS accommodation Medium secure units High security units

6.9 Within these options, purchasers will want to identify and evaluate the appropriate balance in delivering acute and continuing care for their locality. A fuller description of these service settings, highlighting key issues, is given at Appendix 6.1 to assist purchasers in this process. Some research information supporting the effectiveness of different service settings is at Appendix 6.2.

Treatment methods

6.10 A wide range of interventions are available to supplement traditional uses of psychiatry. Controlled evaluation of many psychosocial treatments, particularly cognitive and behavioural psychotherapies and family intervention strategies, have demonstrated their effectiveness in treating mental illness, complementing pharmacological interventions. Comprehensive reviews are readily available of the increasing range of treatments and their appropriate applications. Some examples are given in Appendix 6.3, particularly of:

- psychotherapies
- drug treatments
- ECT.

6.11 Drug treatment with benzodiazepines can be effective in relieving anxiety in the short term. However:

- their effectiveness decreases over time
- long-term use can lead to dependency
- they can mask the underlying symptoms of depression which may then remain untreated.

6.12 A managed move to effective treatments such as anxiety management techniques, relaxation training and psychotherapies needs to be undertaken, particularly in primary health care settings.

Mental illness in general medical and surgical settings

6.13 The incidence of mental health problems is considerably raised amongst people referred to general medical and surgical services. There are a number of reasons for this. Physical health problems, with their associated pain, fear and disability, can cause depression and anxiety. Sometimes people with depression and anxiety are misdiagnosed, leading to unnecessary referrals to general medical and surgical services. And physical and psychiatric problems tend to coexist, for reasons that are not fully understood. Mental health services can relieve suffering and reduce disability (see Appendix 6.4). There is also evidence that the costs of providing high quality liaison psychiatry services is more than matched by the savings made in the reduction of inappropriate investigations and length of stay.

Interventions to reduce suicides

6.15 Suicide is preventable. Lives can be saved. There is a growing body of research on effective interventions which can reduce suicide rates, some of which are highlighted in Appendix 6.5. Evidence suggests that multi-faceted approaches are most successful.

Early Intervention

6.15 Identifying mental illness in its early stages can have a significant effect on hospitalisation and suicide rates. Early identification and management of depression in primary and social care settings – and, in particular, improved management of depression in general practice – have been shown to be effective in reducing suicide rates. The Defeat Depression campaign, being run by the Royal Colleges of General Practitioners and Psychiatrists, should have a significant impact. FHSAs can support the dissemination of materials and its implementation at practice level. Reassessment of services for those who have attempted suicide or parasuicide might usefully be considered in accordance with HC(84)25. People who have attempted suicide in the past are at greatly increased risk – they are approximately 100 times more likely than average to commit suicide in the year after an attempt.

6.16 Provider units will also wish to ensure improved assessment and management of suicide risk in A&E departments, medical and surgical wards by providing training and supervision for front-line staff.

Reducing the availability and access to methods of suicide

6.17 Reductions in access to easy means of lethal injury have been shown to have a marked effect on reducing suicides, reductions which have not been fully compensated for by the substitution of other methods. Changes in car exhaust emission standards in 1992 and the requirement that all new cars be fitted with catalytic converters from January 1993 should help to reduce the incidence of suicide, in line with the experience of other countries where similar changes have already taken place. The NHS can more directly address issues such as labelling, for example to warn of toxicity; restricting the quantities of drugs such as paracetamol that can be supplied at any one time; the use of blister-packs; and the storage and availability of other over the counter medicines which are poisonous.

Appropriately targeted local services

6.18 Evidence suggests an association of lower suicide rates amongst the severely mentally ill with services provided locally by DGHs compared with large mental hospitals. In addition, early research also suggests that the introduction of community-based services can reduce suicide levels. Research has highlighted the hitherto unrecognised frequency of suicide in traditional services. These encouraging findings can be improved upon through careful targeting of those most at risk.

Effective supervision

6.19 The term supervision is one users may be suspicious of, suggesting surveillance and interference with independence and civil liberties. There is a need to combine sensitivity towards service users with the provision of effective care of those who are at high risk of suicide. The ready availability of admission facilities is important in these cases. Within these facilities, there should be clearly defined policies for managing suicidal patients, including defined observation policies.

Discharge from Hospital

6.20 Individuals recently discharged from hospital are at particular risk of attempting suicide. The importance therefore of co-ordinated discharge planning can hardly be overstressed in this context. The Department's Guidance on the discharge of mentally disordered people and their continuing care in the community (HSG(94)27) sets out good practice which should be followed for all patients who are discharged following referral to the specialist mental health services. The Guidance stresses that no person should be discharged from hospital unless those taking that decision are satisfied that he or she can live safely in the community. The assessment of risk in this context is discussed at length. The Guidance also makes clear that in the event of a serious incident local management should investigate to identify any lessons to be learnt. **In the case of a homicide by a mentally ill person it will always be necessary to hold an inquiry which is independent of the providers involved.**

6.21 NHS professionals and provider unit managers should ensure, in collaboration with their personal social services colleagues, that this guidance is put into immediate effect, and that guidelines are put in place which give the necessary priority to meeting the needs of the most severely mentally ill people. Purchasers should secure, not later than 1995/6, the necessary service provision to support the aims of this guidance through the contracting process.

MENTAL ILLNESS

Key Area Handbook

6.22 Copies of HSG(94)27 can be obtained by writing to BAPS, Health Publications Unit, DSS Distribution Centre, Heywood Stores, Manchester Road, Heywood, Lancs. OL10 2PZ.

References
Children and adolescents
KURTZ, Z. (Ed) (1992) *With Health in mind: mental health care for children and young people.* London: Action for Sick Children.
Elderly people
HEALTH ADVISORY SERVICE (1982) *The Rising Tide. Developing services for mental illness in old age.* Surbiton: HAS.
Specialist services
ACCESS TO HEALTH (1992) *Purchasing and providing services for homeless people.* London: Access to Health.
BRIDGES, K., HUXLEY, P. & OLIVER J. Psychiatric rehabilitation: redefined for the 1990s. *International Journal of Social Psychiatry*, (in press).
CREED, F., MAYOU, R & HOPKINS, A. (1992) *Medical symptoms not explained by organic disease.* London: RCPhysicians & RCPsych.
PARRY G. (1992) Improving psychotherapy services: applications of research, audit and evaluation. *British Journal of Clinical Psychology*, **31**, 3-19.
ROYAL COLLEGE OF PSYCHIATRISTS (1992) *Report on Puerperal Mental Illness Services. Council Report* London: R C Psych.
ROYAL COLLEGE OF PSYCHIATRISTS (1992) *Eating Disorders. Council Report* London: R C Psych.
Suicide
APPLEBY, L. (1992) Suicide in psychiatric patients: risk and prevention. *British Journal of Psychiatry*, **161**, 749-758.
BLACKER, C.V.R. et al (1992). Assessment of deliberate self harm on medical wards. *Psychiatric Bulletin*, **16**, 262-263.
HAWTON, K. (1987) Assessment of suicide risk. *British Journal of Psychiatry*, **150**, 145-153.
HEALTH ADVISORY SERVICE. (1994) *Suicide Prevention: the challenge confronted.* London: HMSO.
JENKINS, R. (1994) *The prevention of suicide.* London: HMSO.
MORGAN, H.G. (1992) Suicide prevention. Hazards on the fast lane to community care. *British Journal of Psychiatry*, **160**, 149-153
MORGAN, H.G. & OWEN, J.H. (1990) *Persons at risk of suicide. Guidelines on good clinical practice.* Nottingham: Boots.
MORGAN, H.G. & PRIEST, P. (1991) Suicide and other unexpected deaths among psychiatric in-patients. The Bristol confidential inquiry. *British Journal of Psychiatry*, **158**, 368-374.
ROSSITER, J.C. (1989) Suicidal patients – effect on staff. *Psychiatric Bulletin*, **13**, 495-6.
WORLD HEALTH ORGANISATION (1993) *Guidelines for the primary prevention of mental, neurological and psychosocial disorders, 4: Suicide.* Geneva: WHO.
Supervision
DEPARTMENT OF HEALTH (1993) *Legal Powers on the Care of Mentally Ill People in the Community: Report of the Internal Review* London: DH.
DEPARTMENT OF HEALTH (1994) *The discharge from hospital of mentally disordered people and their continuing care in the community.* (HSG(94)27) Heywood: DH.
WEST MIDLANDS RHA (1991) *Report of the Panel of Inquiry Appointed to Investigate the Case of Kim Kirkman* Birmingham: WMRHA.
NETRHA/SETRHA (1994) *The Report of the Inquiry into the Care and Treatment of Christopher Clunis.* London: HMSO.

SERVICE SETTINGS FOR THE DELIVERY OF MENTAL HEALTH CARE AND TREATMENT

User's homes

1. Most patients can be supported in their homes during periods of crisis, and this is generally their preference. Home care is unsuitable for those at significant risk to themselves or others, and people who live in markedly adverse social circumstances. Individual assessment at home can also be a cost-effective measure, by reducing the likelihood of inappropriate admissions.

Day hospitals

2. These provide alternatives to hospitalisation for even quite psychotic patients, and are suitable settings for group therapies and more intensive support for out-patients. Most patients attend for short periods of up to three months.

Crisis accommodation

3. This can be sited in various settings such as mental health centres, hostels or ordinary housing. The concept is extremely popular with users.

Acute Units

4. Where patients are disturbed or suicidal, a ward's protective environment assists in stabilisation, treatment and reestablishment in the community. Acute units can also be places of sanctuary for vulnerable patients and provide respite for relatives. Many beds are inappropriately occupied, for example by people with severe mental illness awaiting supported accommodation in the community, leaving shortages for use by those in an acute phase of mental illness.

5. Alternatives to location on District General Hospital sites – which may have poor access, be excessively large and in design more suited to general medicine or surgery – can be developed offering a more user-friendly design. Local acute units exist, for example, at The Grange, Long Benton in Newcastle and are being developed, eg in East Birmingham.

Day centres

6. These provide rehabilitation and continuing support. They should be provided in

separate locations to day hospital services, but with close links between them, and integrated with community mental health services as far as possible.

Drop-in centres

7.   Drop-in facilities can allow social contact to be gradually increased and engagement with services commenced.

Community Mental Health/Resource Centres

8.   These can provide local team bases including, where appropriate, interview facilities and day care. Such centres can also provide bases for day care, clubs, adult education, advocacy and other schemes.

Unstaffed group homes/flatlets

9.   Group homes with communal living, for example Housing Association Special Needs Schemes, are an option for some patients who have good relationships with each other. Care managers/key-workers need to ensure that monitoring of the support provided, such as by domiciliary home care workers, occurs on a regular basis.

Adult placement schemes

10.   Such schemes have provided alternative care for a small well-selected group of patients. The importance of selection of carers and patients, training and continuing support, particularly in emergencies, is crucial to the success of such schemes.

11.   If private board and lodging houses are used for accommodation, purchasers should ensure that:

- they are close to friends, family or the user's previous residence (eg the hospital where they were living)
- quality standards are monitored on an ongoing basis by the key worker or care manager, with reference to the relevant local authority registration/inspection unit.

Residential care homes

12.   Small groups of patients will need the support of group homes with staff present in the homes for extended periods of the day or giving 24 hour cover. In the latter case, sleeping-in staff provide the least restrictive, whilst appropriately supportive, option for a significant number of patients.

13. Some schemes have developed on a core and cluster model with staff from the more highly staffed hostels also supporting those which are more independent.

14. Care homes should be local to friends and families, or to the user's previous residence. Voluntary sector organisations – including Turning Point, Making Space, the Guidepost Trust, Mental After Care Association, and the Richmond Fellowship – have particular experience in this area.

Mental nursing homes

15. These provide asylum or sanctuary care for extended periods. Care should be provided in as domestic a setting as possible. The smaller Registered Mental Nursing Homes may be suitable.

24 hour NHS residences

16. Hospital hostels may be suitable for younger age groups, whilst other NHS accommodation will be needed for continuing health care for the elderly. 24 hour residences tend to be more cost effective than long-stay wards and are more appropriate than 'revolving' users in and out of acute wards.

Local Secure Units

17. These complement general psychiatric units and provide short term care for patients either during acutely disturbed episodes, or as part of a rehabilitation plan in levels of progressively less security. Failure to provide sufficient places in these units leads to blocking and unsuitable (and probably more costly) placements elsewhere. Purchasers should, as a priority, assess the need for such places and ensure that a sufficient number are available.

Medium Secure Units

18. These provide care and treatment in conditions of security for patients who are not such a risk as to require a place in a high security unit. Failure to assess and provide the number of places required leads to unsuitable placements in the special hospitals, in

less secure provision or in prison. Purchasers have the formal responsibility placed on the NHS 20 years ago for ensuring that suitable facilities are available for the treatment, care and security needs of their populations.

High Security Units

19. Purchasers should be involved in care planning of all their patients in the special hospitals from admission through to discharge, including, in particular, the placement within 6 months of special hospital patients who no longer need high security facilities. They are under a duty to ensure that the Care Programme Approach is implemented on discharge or transfer to more local services. In addition, they should assess their patients individually to establish their need for high security or alternative care.

Independent Health Care Providers

20. The independent sector offers a range of mental health services, including brain injury rehabilitation, secure units for mentally ill offenders, long-term psychiatric services, adolescent psychiatry, behavioural treatment, 24 hour crisis intervention and drug and substance misuse treatment.

References
Domiciliary management
BARTLETT, N. (1990) Stepping into the breach. *Community Care,* **797,** 14-15.
DEAN, C., PHILLIPS, J., GADD, E.M. et al (1993) Comparison of community based service with hospital based service for people with acute severe psychiatric illness. *British Medical Journal,* **307,** 473-6.
GOOD PRACTICES IN MENTAL HEALTH. *Crisis Services Information Pack.* London: GPMH.
JONES, S.J., TURNER, R.J. & GRANT, J.E. (1987) Assessing patients in their homes. *Bulletin of the Royal College of Psychiatrists,* **11,** 117-9.
KATSCHNIG, H., KONIECZNA, T. & COOPER J.E. (1993) *Emergency psychiatric and crisis intervention services in Europe.* Geneva: World Health Organisation.

Crisis accommodation
TURKINGTON, D., *et al.* (1991) The use of an unstaffed flat for crisis intervention and rehabilitation. *Psychiatric Bulletin,* **15,** 13-14.

Acute units
MEDICAL ARCHITECTURE RESEARCH UNIT (1991) *Building for mental health.* London: PNL Press.
DEPARTMENT OF HEALTH NHS ESTATES DIVISION (1993) *Design Guide. Accommodation for adults with acute mental illness – options for the 90's.* London: HMSO.
PECK, E. & SCOTT, J. (1990) Myth and Reality. *Health Services Journal,* **100,** 365.

Local secure unit
BLUMENTHAL, S. & WESSLEY, S. (June 1992) The Extent of Local Arrangements for the Diversion of the Mentally Abnormal Offender from Custody. A Report to the Department of Health.
HAYES, G. & SOLIMAN, A. (1991) The development of a district based forensic service. *Psychiatric Bulletin,* **15,** 149-150.
O'GRADY, J.C, (1990) The complementary role of regional and local secure provision for psychiatric patients: three years experience in Leeds. *Health Trends,* **22,** 14-16.

Care management
CHALLIS, D., CHESTERMAN, J., TRASKE, K & VON ABENDORFF, R. (1987) Assessment and case management: some cost implications. *Social Work and Social Sciences Review,* **1,** 3, 147-162.
HUXLEY, P.H. (August 10 1990) Community mental health: a way of meeting the challenge. *Community Psychiatric Nursing,* **4,** 13-19.
LAMB, H.R. (1980) Therapist case-managers: more than brokers of services. *Hospital and Community Psychiatry,* **31,** 14-18.
ONYETT, S. (1982) *Case management in mental health.* London: Chapman & Hall

Day care

ECHLIN, R. (1990) *Day Care Information Pack*. London: GPMH.

VAUGHAN, P.J. & PRECHNER, M. (June 1985) Occupation or therapy in psychiatric day care? *Occupational Therapy*, 169-171

KINGDON, D.G. *et al.* (1989) Befriending: cost-effective community care. *Psychiatric Bulletin*, **13,** 350-351.

PYM, B. (6 April 1989) Run it your own way. *Community Care*, 17-19.

Residential accommodation

ANSTEE, B.H. (1985) An alternative form of community care for the mentally ill: supported lodging schemes...a personal view. *Health Trends*, **17,** 39-40.

HAMMOND, T & WALLACE, P. (1991) *Housing for people who are severely mentally ill*. London: National Schizophrenia Fellowship.

MIND (1992) *Housing with support: a quality action guide*. LONDON: MIND.

RESEARCH AND DEVELOPMENT FOR PSYCHIATRY (1992) *Who does what?* London: RDP.

SHERLOCK, J. (1991) *At home in the community*. London: GPMH.

DEPARTMENT OF HEALTH SOCIAL SERVICES INSPECTORATE (1991) *All change*. London: DH SSI.

DEPARTMENT OF HEALTH SOCIAL SERVICES INSPECTORATE (1993) *Guidance on Standards for Short-term Breaks*. London: HMSO.

DEPARTMENT OF HEALTH SOCIAL SERVICES INSPECTORATE (1993) *Standards for the Residential Care of Elderly People with Mental Disorders*. London: HMSO.

DEPARTMENT OF HEALTH SOCIAL SERVICES INSPECTORATE (1992) *Standards for specialist residential care for people with mental health problems*. London: HMSO.

DEPARTMENT OF HEALTH SOCIAL SERVICES INSPECTORATE (1993) *No longer afraid – the safeguard of older people in domestic settings*. London: DH.

WING, J.K. & FURLONG, R. (1986) A haven for the severely disabled within the context of a comprehensive psychiatric Service. *British Journal of Psychiatry*, **14,** 449-457.

YOUNG, R. (Ed) (1992) *Residential needs for severely disabled psychiatric patients*. London: HMSO.

Appendix 6.2

EVALUATION OF DIFFERENT SERVICE SETTINGS FOR THE TREATMENT OF PEOPLE WITH MENTAL ILLNESS

This appendix briefly outlines evaluations of different service settings.

Comparison of services

1. GRAD, J. & SAINSBURY, P. (1963) Evaluating a community care service. *Trends in the Mental Health Services* (Ed Freeman & Farndale J.) London: Pergamon.

   This comparison of an early community service with a more traditional one concluded that hospital admissions were reduced in number in the former. However whilst this markedly increased burden on families, admissions were more likely to be appropriately responding to social pressures and the domestic problems of patients' families who generally preferred the community services.

2. BEISER, M., SHORE, J.H., PETERS, R. & TATUM, E. (1985) Does community care for the mentally ill make a difference? A tale of two cities. *American Journal of Psychiatry,* **142,** 1047-52.

   Matched groups of schizophrenic patients were assessed over a period of one year following discharge in two cities, one with and one without 'model' community services. The former experienced fewer admissions, were more likely to be employed, and reported a higher level of well-being.

3. HAFNER, H. & KLUG, P. (1982) Effectiveness and cost of community care for schizophrenic patients. *Hospital and Community Psychiatry,* **40,** 59-63.

   Changes in utilisation of psychiatric services, following a change from a hospital-centred to an integrated community-based structure, were found to cover needs previously unmet, particularly alcohol-related disorders and depression, at similar cost.

Components of services

4. JONES, R., GOLDBERG, D. & HUGHES (1980) A comparison of two different services treating schizophrenia: a cost benefit approach. *Psychological Medicine,* **10,** 493-505.

   Comparisons were made over a four year period between patients admitted with schizophrenia to a teaching District General Hospital unit and to an Area Mental

Hospital with modern rehabilitation facilities. Clinical outcomes were broadly similar but the former imposed less of a strain on relatives and was associated with less unmet need. Duration of stay was also significantly shorter and, despite higher unit costs, the DGH(T) was economically superior to the Area Mental Hospital.

5.   TYRER, P. *et al* (1989) Integrated hospital and community psychiatric services and use of inpatient beds. *British Medical Journal,* **299,** 298–300.

Introducing community services with specific geographical boundaries in Nottingham led to a significant reduction in admissions and overall use of inpatient beds. It was concluded that such 'sectorisation' was a viable and economic way of improving psychiatric services.

6.   KNAPP, M. *et al* (1990) The TAPS project 3: Predicting the community costs of closing psychiatric hospitals. *British Journal of Psychiatry,* **157,** 661–70.

The team for the assessment of psychiatric services was established in 1985 to monitor closure of Friern and Claybury Hospitals in North East Thames and a series of publications have resulted. Community costs for replacement services have been found to be lower than hospital costs, not just for the first cohorts of leavers, and are predicted to remain so for the full populations of the two hospitals. Users generally prefer the new services.

7.   YOUNG, R. [Ed] (1991) *Residential needs for severely disabled psychiatric patients: the case for hospital hostels*. London: HMSO.

HYDE, C., BRIDGES, K., GOLDBERG, D. *et al* (1987) The evaluation of a hostel ward. *British Journal of Psychiatry,* **151,** 805–12.

These studies demonstrate that domestic accommodation with 24 hour nurse staffing (hospital hostels) can provide alternative residential provision for those with severe mental illness who were previously accommodated in 'long-stay wards'. Costs tend to be less. They can provide more appropriate placement than 'revolving' in and out of acute wards as has been seen in many districts, particularly in London.

8.   CREED, F. *et al* (1990) Randomised controlled trial of day patient versus inpatient psychiatric treatment. *British Medical Journal,* **300,** 1033–7.

DICK, P. *et al* (1985) Day and full-time psychiatric treatment: a controlled comparison. *British Journal of Psychiatry*, **47**, 246-50.

> Day hospital care is an effective alternative to admission for most neurotic and personality disordered patients and many psychotic ones. Length of stay in day hospitals has tended to be longer, off-setting some of the cost-savings made.

9. BURTON, A., WEISBROD, A., TEST, M.A. & STEIN, L.I. (1980) Alternative to mental hospital III: economic cost-benefit analysis. *Archives of General Psychiatry*, **37**, 400-5.

HOULT, J. & REYNOLDS, I. (1984) Schizophrenia: a comparative trial of community orientated and hospital orientated psychiatric care. *Acta Psychiatrica Scandinavica*, **69**, 359-72.

DEAN, C. & GADD, E. (1991) Home treatment for acute psychiatric illness. *British Medical Journal*, **301**, 1021-3.

MERSON, S. *et al* (1992) Early intervention in psychiatric emergencies: a controlled clinical trial. *Lancet*, **339**, 1311-4.

> Providing intensive treatment and support to acutely ill patients and their carers has been shown in a number of studies to be not only cost-effective but also preferred by patients and carers. Patients usually excluded have been those at significant risk to self, or others or in markedly adverse social circumstances. Long-term sustainability of intensive home support schemes has yet to be demonstrated in the UK.

10. CORNEY, R. & CLARE, A. (1983) The effectiveness of attached social workers in the management of depressed women in General Practice. *British Journal of Social Work*, **13**, 57-74.

> With appropriate training, social workers have been shown to be effective in helping people with depression.

11. BURNS, T., BEARDSMORE A., BHAT A.V., OLIVER A. & MATHERS C. (1993) A Controlled Trial of Home-based Acute Psychiatric Services. I: Clinical and Social Outcome. *British Journal of Psychiatry*, **163**, 49-54.

BURNS T., RAFTERY J., BEARDSMORE A., McGUIGAN S., & DICKSON M. (1993) A Controlled Trial of Home-based Acute Psychiatric Services. II: Treatment Patterns and Costs. *British Journal of Psychiatry,* **163,** 55-61.

CONWAY, ALISON S., MELZER, DAVID, HALE, ANTHONY S. (1994) The outcome of targeting community mental health services: evidence from the West Lambeth schizophrenia cohort. *British Medical Journal,* **308,** 627-630.

Working in a multidisciplinary way is cost-effective, especially by reducing admissions to hospital. Targeting community teams on those who are severely mentally ill can reduce symptoms. Both studies produced encouraging, though very preliminary, signs that suicide rates may also be reduced.

Appendix 6.3

EVALUATION OF PSYCHIATRIC TREATMENT METHODS

Psychotherapies

1. Controlled evaluation of family, behavioural and cognitive therapies have demonstrated their effectiveness in a wide variety of conditions including schizophrenia, depression, anxiety, phobias, obsessional neurosis and bulimia. Further evaluation is needed of other psychotherapies to fully interpret their most appropriate use. A wide range of studies on these is described in Milton below.

ANDREWS, G. (1991) The evaluation of psychotherapy. *Current Opinion in Psychiatry,* **4,** 379-83.

CRAIGHEAD, L.W. & CRAIGHEAD, W.E. (1991) Behaviour therapy: recent developments. *Current Opinion in Psychiatry,* **4,** 916-20.

MILTON, J. [Ed] (1992) *Presenting the case for psychoanalytic psychotherapy services. An annotated bibliography.* London: Association for Psychoanalytic Psychotherapy in the NHS, Tavistock Centre, 120 Belsize Lane, London, NW3 5BA.

Drug treatments

2. Drug treatments are well established and demonstrably effective in many conditions notably depression and schizophrenia.

MONTGOMERY, S. (1982) Antidepressant drugs. *Recent Advances in Psychiatry,* **4.** [Ed: Granville-Grossman K] London: Churchill Livingstone.

DAVIS, J.M. (1991) The treatment of schizophrenia. *Current Opinion in Psychiatry,* **4,** 28-33.

MELTZER, H., COLA, P., WAY, L., THOMPSON, P., BASTANI, B., DAVIES, M. & SNITZ, B. (1993). Cost effectiveness of clozapine in neuroleptic-resistant schizophrenia. *American Journal of Psychiatry,* **150,** 1630-1638.

ECT

3. ECT has been shown to be effective by controlled evaluations against simulated treatments for depressed people who are retarded (slowed in movements and thought) and/or suffering from delusions.

BUCHAN, H., JOHNSTONE, E., MCPHERSON, K. *et al* (1992) Who benefits from ECT? *British Journal of Psychiatry,* **160,** 355-9.

Care Programme Approach

4.   Studies of case management and team working support the principles of the Care Programme Approach and specific evaluations of it are now emerging. They demonstrate that implementation is not only possible, but leads to lower readmission rates after index admissions which may be longer, less use of the Mental Health Act, reduced rent arrears and less police involvement:

PIERIDES, M., ROY, D. & CRAIG, T. (1994) The Care Programme Approach. Preliminary results one year after implementation in an inner city hospital. *Psychiatric Bulletin,* 18,4,249. (Report in correspondence.)

TYRER, P. *et al* (1994) *Report to North West Thames RHA on implementation of the care programme approach.* NWTRHA: London.

MENTAL DISORDER IN GENERAL MEDICAL AND SURGICAL SETTINGS

A number of studies have described the high levels of mental disorder in general medical and surgical settings. There is now a growing body of evidence demonstrating that psychiatric interventions can have a beneficial effect, for example in:

- reducing lengths of stay in hospital wards
- reducing admission rates to hospital, for example for children with asthma
- reducing coronary risk
- improving outcomes for elderly people with hip fractures and women with irritable bowel syndrome

ACKERMAN, A.D., LYONS, J.S., HAMMER, J.S. *et al* (1988) The impact of co-existing depression and timing of psychiatric consultation on medical patients' length of stay. *Hospital and Community Psychiatry,* **39,** 173-6.

BROWN, A. & COOPER, A.F. (1987) The impact of a liaison psychiatry service on patterns of referral in a General Hospital. *British Journal of Psychiatry,* **150,** 83-7.

GLASS, R., MULVIHILL, M., SMITH, H. *et al* (1978) The 4 score: an index for predicting a patient's non-medical hospital days. *American Journal of Public Health,* **8,** 751-5.

LEVITAN, S.J. & KORNFIELD, D.S. (1981) Clinical and cost benefits of liaison psychiatry. *American Journal of Psychiatry,* **138,** 790-3.

HOCHSTADT, N., SHEPARD, J. & LULLA, S.H. (1980) Reducing hospitalisation of children with asthma. *Journal of Paediatrics,* **97,** 1012-5.

MUMFORD, E., SCHLESINGER, H.J., GLASS *et al* (1984) A new look at evidence about reduced cost of medical utilisation following mental health treatment. *American Journal of Psychiatry,* **141,** 1145-58.

PATEL, C., MARMOT, M.G., TERRY, D.J. *et al* (1985) Trial of relaxation in reducing coronary risk: four year follow-up. *British Medical Journal,* **290,** 1103-6.

STRAIN, J.J., LYONS, J.S., HAMMER, J.S. *et al* (1991) Cost offset from a psychiatric consultation-liaison intervention with elderly hip fracture patients. *American Journal of Psychiatry,* **148,** 1044-1049.

ZIMMER, J. (1974) Length of stay and hospital bed utilisation. *Medical Care,* **14,** 453-462.

Appendix 6.5

INTERVENTIONS TO REDUCE SUICIDE
A. ASSESSMENT OF INTERVENTIONS
Improved management of depression in general practice

1. RUTZ, W., VON KNORRING, L. & WALINDER, J. (1992) Long-term effects of an educational program for general practitioners given by the Swedish Committee for the prevention and treatment of depression. *Acta Psychiatrica Scandinavica,* **85,** 83-8.

This study demonstrated, amongst other things, significant reductions in hospitalisation and suicide rates in response to the program.

Developing more local services

2. WILLIAMS, P., DE SALVIA, D. & TANSELLA, M. (1987) Suicide and Italian psychiatric reform: an appraisal of two data collection systems. *European Archives of Psychiatry and Neurological Sciences,* **36,** 37-40.

Evidence suggests an association of lower suicide rates with locally provided DGHs compared to areas served by mental hospitals. Some unpublished British evidence also suggests the introduction of community-based services may reduce levels.

Changing availability of means to suicide

3. MARZUK, P.M. *et al* (1992) The effect of access to lethal methods of injury on suicidal rates. *Archives of General Psychiatry,* **49,** 451-8.

KREITMAN, N. (1976) The coal gas story: UK suicide rates 1960-71. *British Journal of Preventative & Social Medicine,* **30,** 86-93.

The ready availability of lethal methods of injury, eg firearms, barbiturates, coal gas, appears to increase suicide rates. When access is reduced or removed (for example when coal gas was replaced by natural gas) the use of other methods of suicide does not appear to increase to compensate. Hence a sustained fall in suicides occurs.

4. CLARKE, R.V. & LESTER, D. (1987) Toxicity of car exhaust and opportunity for suicide: comparison between Britain and the United States. *Journal of Epidemiology and Community Health,* **41,** 114–20.

TARBUCK, A.F. & O'BRIEN, J.T. (1992) Suicide and vehicle exhaust emissions. *British Medical Journal,* **304,** 1376.

Changes in car exhaust emission standards in the US in 1968 led to a reduction in deaths from exhaust fumes not seen in the UK. Similar controls introduced on 1st January 1992 in the UK and the requirement that new cars be fitted with catalytic converters from 1st January 1993 can be expected to have a similar effect, increasing over time.

CHAPTER 7

TARGETING RESOURCES ON SEVERELY MENTALLY ILL PEOPLE

TARGETING RESOURCES ON SEVERELY MENTALLY ILL PEOPLE

Action Summary

DHAs (and GPFHs), FHSAs, SSDs, NHS Trusts

▋ Build up a composite picture of the needs of severely mentally ill people in the area

DHAs (and GPFHs) and SSDs

▋ Target resources towards severely mentally ill people through the contracting process.

NHS Trusts

▋ Identify severely mentally ill people in the area, and ensure that they receive priority for care and follow-up.

▋ Liaise with FHSAs and primary care to support PHCTs in caring for minor psychiatric morbidity.

FHSAs

▋ Develop a strategy with local PHCTs to support primary care in caring for minor psychiatric morbidity.

Why target mental health services?

7.1 There is now widespread agreement that people who are most disabled by mental illness should be afforded the highest priority, and that services should be provided in relation to need. There is evidence that in some areas resources are not currently matched to need, and that some vulnerable individuals may be neglected. It is therefore important in planning and providing specialist mental health services to have a clear view about how to put this policy into practice. These issues are addressed in this chapter.

Defining priority groups

7.2   The most disabled group of patients are often referred to as 'severely mentally ill' (SMI), but there is no widely agreed definition of SMI. Some of the most useful definitions are given in Table (★1). In many local areas a working definition is reached pragmatically, based, for example, on agreed priorities for local rehabilitation, or perhaps care management services.

7.3   It should be recognized that diagnostic groups have serious limitations in predicting need and service usage. People with chronic neuroses for example can have needs as great as patients suffering from schizophrenia and affective psychosis. *The Health of the Nation* Outcome Scales can be expected to assist in producing a more robust definition of severe mental illness, when they become widely available.

Identifying target groups in practice

7.4   In clinical practice, general adult mental health services will need to distinguish high priority referrals and continuing care cases from others. The guidelines in Table (★2) set out one practical method to perform such triage, on the basis of the level of support needed by each patient. Patient needs will change over time, and so the level of support category that each patient is given will need to be regularly reviewed.

7.5   In some areas a proportion of people disabled by severe mental illness will not be in contact with specialist or other services. It may be useful, therefore, to undertake a case identification exercise locally to establish the need for specialist mental health services. Table (★3) shows possible sources of information to use in undertaking this type of needs assessment exercise.

Table (*1) Definitions of the Severely Mentally Ill

1. Goldman, (1981)	

1. Goldman, (1981)

   A **Diagnosis:** patients diagnosed according to DSM-III-R criteria with these 3 conditions:

      Schizophrenia and schizo-affective disorder   (ICD9 295)
      bipolar disorders and major depression   (ICD9 296)
      delusional (paranoid) disorder   (ICD9 297)

   B **Duration** at least one year since onset of disorder

   C **Disability** sufficient to seriously impair functioning of role performance in at least one of the following areas:

      occupation
      family responsibilities
      accommodation

2. McLean & Liebowitz (1989)

At least one of the following must be present:

1. two or more years contact with services
2. depot prescribed
3. ICD9 295 or 297
4. 3 or more inpatient admissions in the last 2 years
5. 3 or more day-patient episodes in the last 2 years
6. DSM-III-R highest level of adaptive functioning in the past year level 5 or less

3. Tyrer (1991)

Patients with chronic psychosis
Two/more in-patient admissions in the past year
Contact with two/more psychiatric agencies in past year
Frequent consultations
Risk of being imprisoned

4. Derived from Patmore & Weaver (1990)

   A Psychotic diagnosis, organic illness or injury AND previous compulsory admission OR aggregate one year stay in hospital in past five years OR three or more admissions in past five years

   B Psychotic diagnosis, organic illness or injury OR any previous admissions in past five years

   C No record of Hospital admissions AND
      No recorded psychotic diagnosis, organic illness or injury

Table (*2) Guidelines to Distinguish High, Medium and Low Support Mental Health Services

Group	Patient Characteristics	CPA	Supervision Register
High support group	Individuals with severe social dysfunction (eg social isolation support unemployment, and/or difficulty with skills of daily living) as a consequence of severe or persistent mental illness or disorder. In particular, individuals with the following difficulties will be identified for high levels of support: ● current or recent serious risk to self or to others or of self-neglect ● severe behavioural difficulties ● high risk of relapse ● history of poor engagement with mental health services ● little contact with other providers of care ● precarious housing (eg bed & breakfast) ● need staff : patient ratio of about 1:15	√	?√
Medium support group	Individuals with a moderate degree of social disability arising from mental illness or disorder, eg those able to work at least part-time and/or to maintain at least one enduring relationship. This group will also include the following individuals: ● those likely to recognise, and to seek help when early in relapse ● those receiving appropriate services from other agencies	√	X
Low support group	Individuals who, following assessment, have been found to have specific and limited mental health-related needs which do not require extensive, multi-disciplinary input. In general, such individuals are likely to respond to brief or low-intensity intervention. For example: ● patients with psychosis in remission ● moderately severe personality disorder	√	X

Table (*3) Sources of local information on SMI patients

1.	**Patients using Mental Health Services** Outpatient attenders CPN case-load and depot clinic patients Mental Health Act data Domiciliary visit records Crisis attenders and Accident and Emergency Department attenders In-patient audit data Residents of long-stay institutions
2.	**Patients using Primary Care Services only** Past diagnosis of psychosis Repeat psychotropic drug prescriptions Frequent emergency and other consultations CPN attenders
3.	**Patients using Social Services** Area social worker case-loads Hostel/group home/sheltered residence populations Care management recipients Housing Department clients causing concern
4.	**Patients using Voluntary Sector and other Agencies** Residents of sheltered accommodation Individuals presenting to churches in distress Imprisoned and homeless patients Probation officer case-loads Drop-in and other casual facility users

Developing services for people disabled by severe mental illness.

7.6 To enable people who are seriously disabled by mental illness to have choice in the services which may help them, a reasonable range of facilities should be made available in each local area. Table (*4) sets out the types of facility which will usually be needed.

7.7 Targeting services in the way suggested does mean that both nursing and other managers and consultants will need to review and prioritize referrals and case loads, to ensure that people at greater need take precedence over others. This may affect waiting times and require the use of brief interventions, including self-help techniques, for those whose needs are less great. Staff will need to be available to act rapidly in response to urgent referrals, and to meet the needs of patients relapsing, being discharged, or discharging themselves from in patient settings.

Table (*4) Ten Core Components of a Comprehensive Mental Health Service (see also chapter 6, and appendix 6.1 above)

1.	Case registers (from Care Programme Approach and Supervision Register)
2.	Crisis response services
3.	Hospital and community places
4.	Assertive outreach and care management services
5.	Day care
6.	Assessment and consultation services
7.	Carer and community education and support
8.	Primary care liaison
9.	Physical and dental care
10.	User advocacy and community alliances

Bed management strategies

7.8 In services where there are good bed management strategies, inappropriate admissions can often be prevented:

- **Organisation of service:** sectorisation of psychiatric services allows organisation of the psychiatric services for the whole population

- **Site of assessment:** initial assessment being undertaken at home. Where assessments take place at the site of the acute beds, the likelihood of inappropriate admission is increased.

- **Senior gate-keeping:** where senior doctors or nurses are constantly involved in any decision to admit a patient, their ability to make a more informed decision and to judge risks more accurately decreases hospital admissions.

- **Bed manager:** in services where an experienced nurse provides a triage function, bed use is likely to be decreased.

- **Discharge planning:** in the event of a homeless person being admitted, if priority is placed on immediate referral to housing services, inappropriate and extended use of beds can be prevented. The referral process should begin with admission.

- **Continuity of care:** most readmissions and suicide attempts occur in the first 4-6 weeks after discharge. Outpatient appointments may be appropriately given within this timescale rather than at a later stage. Any follow-up by key workers, case managers, care managers, mental health nurses or others is more likely to be successful if it is intensive in this vulnerable period.

- **Urgent out-patient services:** urgent out-patient appointments and community team assessments must be available as part of a comprehensive service to reduce the need for in-patient admission.

- **Integrated hospital and community services:** research has demonstrated that without an integrated approach where community teams have control over their own hospital beds, both bed use and length of stay are significantly increased and continuity of care is decreased.

- **Leave beds:** each unit should have an agreed policy on how many beds should be held for patients on leave or absent without leave.

- **Audit of bed usage:** regular peer audit of admissions can improve management and use of community facilities.

- **Nurse-staffed community accommodation:** many patients spend excessive periods on acute wards. Nurse-staffed hostels can provide more appropriate rehabilitation, respite and sanctuary.

Mental health care in primary care

7.9 While specialist mental health services should target people with the severest forms of mental illness, it is important to note that the vast majority of people with mental illness suffers from less disabling problems. There are approximately 30,000 GPs in the country, each of whom will have 300-600 patients with depression and anxiety in any one year, but fewer than 2,000 consultant psychiatrists. Therefore each psychiatrist needs to have close links with at least 15 GPs, and could realistically only help each GP with a tiny handful of their depressed patients. Therefore patients not suffering from severe mental illness are usually most appropriately seen in primary care.

7.10 Similarly, there is one community mental health nurse to between five and ten GPs (the precise ratio varying across the country). If we take the best case of one community mental health nurse to every five GPs, we know that on average, each GP has seven patients with chronic severe mental illness (mostly chronic schizophrenia) who require the supervision, support, family interventions, etc from the community mental health nurse (Kendrick, 1991). He or she thus already should have a caseload of 35. It is easy to see that if each GP also refers three or four depressed patients, the community mental health nurse's working week has been overloaded (unless care is withdrawn from those with severe mental illness) and, meanwhile, only a tiny dent has been made on the GP's load of several hundred depressed patients.

7.11 The severely mentally ill now, more than ever, need concentrated efforts in continuing care during and after they leave hospital. Community mental health nurses will often be their case managers and/or key workers, and there are substantial concerns that this important work is being jeopardised by the shift of community mental health nurse caseloads from being primarily focused on the severely mentally ill to being primarily focused on those with minor psychiatric morbidity (White, 1990).

The range of mental health services in primary care

7.12 To provide a comprehensive service at the primary care level, a range of contributions from different specialists is necessary.

Counsellors

7.13 The growth of counsellors in general practice is now well established, and current research is investigating the effectiveness of the brief psychotherapies used by counsellors, the indications for such treatment, the side effects, ethical and training issues, and their use in relation to other members of the primary care team.

Practice Nurses

7.14 Most GPs already employ practice nurses, but these have traditionally only been used for physical and not psychological problems. However, there are now a number of innovative studies of using practice nurses for psychological problems.

Health visitors and District Nurses

7.15 These staff are in the frontline of primary care and have a particular role in the detection of depression in young mothers and in the elderly, and in supporting and treating them.

GP Facilitators

7.16 The GP facilitator is a relatively recently developed role. He or she will help general practices to develop protocols for the screening and management of mental illness; assist in early detection and prompt treatment of people who are depressed and anxious, in order to avoid the consequences of untreated depression; and identify and support those at risk of depression, eg the elderly, bereaved, socially isolated, physically disabled, the blind and deaf and those with painful, chronic or life threatening disease. Studies are now underway to evaluate the effectiveness of such facilitators.

References

AUDIT COMMISSION (1992) Lying in Wait: The Use of Medical Beds in Acute Hospitals. London: HMSO.

BEBBINGTON, P.E., FEENEY, S., FLANAGHAN, C. (1993) Clinical Audit of Psychiatric Inpatients. In: THORNICROFT, G., BREWIN, C., WING, J.K. (eds) Measuring Mental Health Needs. London: Gaskell.

BIRCHWOOD, M., SMITH, J., MacMILLAN, F., HOGG, B., PRASAD, R., HARVEY, C., BERING, S. (1989) Predicting relapse in schizophrenia: the development and implementation of an early signs monitoring system using patients and families as observers, a preliminary investigation. *Psychological Medicine,* **19:** 649-656.

BROOKER, C. (1990) A new role for the community psychiatric nurse in working with families caring for a relative with schizophrenia. *International Journal of Social Psychiatry,* **36:** 216-24.

BROWN, G.W., BIRLEY, J.L.T., WING, J.K. (1972) Influence of Family Life on the course of Schizophrenic Disorders: a Replication. *British Journal of Psychiatry,* **121:** 241.

BURNS, T., BEADSMORE, A., BHAT, A.V., *et al* (1993) A controlled trial of home based acute psychiatric services 1: clinical and social outcome. *British Journal of Psychiatry,* **163:** 49-54.

CARPENTER, W.T., HEINRICHS, D.W., HANLON, T.E. (1987) A comparative trial of pharmacological strategies in schizophrenia. *American Journal of Psychiatry,* **144:** 1466-1470.

CROW, T.J., MacMILLAN, J.F., JOHNSON, A.L., JOHNSTONE, E.C. (1986). A randomised controlled trial of prophylactic neuroleptic treatment. *British Journal of Psychiatry,* **148:** 120-127.

DEAN, C., PHILLIPS, J., GADD, E.M., *et al* (1993) Comparison of community based service with hospital based service for people with acute severe psychiatric illness. *British Medical Journal,* **307:** 473-476.

DEDMAN, P. (1993) Home treatment for acute psychiatric disorder. *British Medical Journal,* **306:** 1359-1360.

ECKMAN, T., WIRSHING, W.C., MARDER, S.R., *et al* (1992) Technique for training schizophrenic patients in illness self-management: A controlled trial. *American Journal of Psychiatry,* **11:** 1549.

FALLOON, I.R.H., FADDEN, G. (1993) Integrated Mental Health Care: A comprehensive community-based approach. Cambridge: Cambridge University Press.

FALLOON, I.R.H., TALBOT, R.E. (1981) Persistent auditory hallucinations: Coping mechanisms and implications for management. *Psychological Medicine,* **11:** 329.

GOLDMAN, H. (1981). Defining and counting the chronically mentally ill. *Hospital and Community Psychiatry,* **32,** 21-27.

GUNDERSON, J.G., FRANK, A.F., KATZ, H.M., *et al* (1984) Effects of psychotherapy in schizophrenia: II. Comparative outcome of two forms of treatment. *Schizophrenia Bulletin,* **10:** 564.

HARRISON, G., OWENS, D., HOLTON, A., NEILSON, D., BOOT, D. (1988) A prospective study of severe mental disorder in Afro-Caribbean patients. *Psychological Medicine,* **18:** 643-657.

HIRSH, S., *et al* (1988) Psychiatric Beds and Resources: Factors influencing Bed Use and Service Planning. Report of a Working Party of the Section for Social and Community Psychiatry of the Royal College of Psychiatrists. London: Gaskell.

JARMAN, B. (1983) Identification of underprivileged areas. *British Medical Journal,* **256:** 1587-1592.

JOHNSON, S., THORNICROFT, G. Emergency psychiatric services: a review and preview. In: PHELAN, M., STRATHDEE, G., THORNICROFT, G. (eds). Emergency Mental Health Services in the Community. Cambridge: Cambridge University Press (In Press).

JOHNSON, S., THORNICROFT. G (1993) The sectorisation of psychiatric services in England and Wales. *Social Psychiatry and Psychiatric Epidemiology,* **28:** 45-47.

KINGDON, D., TURKINGTON, D., JOHN, C. (1994) Cognitive Behaviour Therapy of Schizophrenia. *British Journal of Psychiatry,* **164:** 581.

LEFF, J., KUIPERS, L., BERKOWITZ, R. *et al* (1982) A controlled trial of social intervention in the families of schizophrenic patients. *British Journal of Psychiatry,* **141:** 121.

McCRONE, P. (1994) Predicting mental health service use: diagnosis based systems and alternatives. *Journal of Mental Health* (In Press).

McLEAN, E., LIEBOWITZ, J. (1989). Towards a working definition of the long-term mentally ill. *Psychiatric Bulletin,* **13,** 251-252.

PATRICK, M., HIGGITT, A., HOLLOWAY, F. (1989) Changes in an inner city psychiatric inpatient service following bed losses: a follow-up of the East Lambeth 1986 Survey *Health Trends,* **21,** 121-123.

OVRETVEIT, J. (1993) Coordinating Community Care. Multidisciplinary teams and care management. Buckingham: Open University Press.

OYNETT, S. (1992) Case management in mental health. London: Chapman and Hall.

PATMORE, C., WEAVER, J. (1990) A Survey of Community Mental Health Centres. London: Good Practice in Mental Health.

PHELAN, M., McCRONE, P. (1994) Psychiatric DRGs in the UK? *Hospital and Community Psychiatry* (In Press).

STEIN, L., TEST, M.A. (1980) Alternative to mental hospital. 1. Conceptual model, treatment programme and clinical evaluation. *Archives of General Psychiatry,* **37:** 392-397.

STRATHDEE, G. and THORNICROFT, G. (1992) Community Sectors for Needs-Led Mental Health Services. In: Measuring Mental Health Needs (THORNICROFT, G., BREWIN, C. and WING, J.K. (eds) Royal College of Psychiatrists. London: Gaskell Press.

STRATHDEE, G., THORNICROFT, G. (1994) Community Psychiatry and Service Evaluation. In MURRAY, R., HILL, P., McGUFFIN, P. (eds). *The Essentials of Psychiatry* (In Press).

SUTHERBY, K., SRINATH, S., STRATHDEE, G. (1992) The domiciliary consultation service: outdated anachronism or essential part of community psychiatric outreach? *Health Trends* **24(3):** 103-105.

TARRIER, N., BECKETT, R., HARWOOD, S., *et al* (1993) A trial of two cognitive-behaviour methods of treating drug-resistant residual psychotic symptoms in schizophrenic patients 1 Outcome. *British Journal of Psychiatry,* **162:** 524.

TYRER, P. (1985) The 'hive' system: a model for a psychiatric service. *British Journal of Psychiatry,* **146:** 571-575.

TYRER, P., TURNER, R., JOHNSON, A.L. (1989) Integrated use of hospital and community psychiatric services and use of inpatient beds. *British Medical Journal,* **299:** 298-300.

VAUGHN, C.F., LEFF, J.P.(1976) Influence of family and social factors on the course of psychiatric illness. *British Journal of Psychiatry,* **129:** 125.

WOOFF, K., GOLDBERG, D.P., FRYERS, T. (1988) The practice of community psychiatric nursing and mental health social work in Salford. Some implications for community care. *British Journal of Psychiatry,* **152:** 783-792.

WOOFF, K., ROSE, S., STREET, J. (1989) Community psychiatric nursing services in Salford, Southampton and Worcester. In Health Service Planning and Research: contributions from case registers. WING, J.K. (ed) London: Gaskell.

Primary Care

CORNEY, R., JENKINS, R. (1992) Counselling in General Practice. London: Routledge.

DEPARTMENT OF HEALTH (1988) On the State of the Public Health. London: HMSO.

DEPARTMENT OF HEALTH (1989) Caring for People, Community Care in the Next Decade and Beyond. London: HMSO.

GOLDBERG, D.P., HUXLEY, P. (1980) Mental Illness in the Community - the pathway to care. London: Tavistock.

JENKINS, R. (1990) Towards a system of outcome indicators for mental health, *British Journal of Psychiatry,* **157,** pp 500-514.

JENKINS, R., FIELD, V., YOUNG, R. (1992) Primary Care of Schizophrenia. London: HMSO.

JENKINS, R., NEWTON, J., YOUNG, R. (1992) Prevention of Depression and Anxiety - the Role of the Primary Care Team. London: HMSO.

KENDRICK, T., SIBBALD, P. BURNS, T., FREELING, P. (1991) Role of general practitioners in care of long-term mentally ill, *British Medical Journal,* **302,** pp 508-510.

PAYKEL, E. (1990) Innovations in mental health care in the primary care system, in: MARKS, I., SCOTT, R. (Eds) Mental Health Care Delivery, pp 69-83. Cambridge: Cambridge University Press.

PENDLETON, T., SCHOFIELD, T., TATE, P., HAVELOCK, P. (1984) The consultation: an approach to hearing and teaching: Oxford General Practice Services 6. Oxford: Oxford University Press.

STRATHDEE, G., WILLIAMS P. (1984) A survey of psychiatrists in primary care: the silent growth of a new service, *Journal of the Royal College of General Practitioners,* **34,** pp 615-618.

WHITE, E. (1990) The Third Quinquennial Survey of Community Psychiatric Nurses. Manchester: Manchester University.

WHO (1973) Primary Care of Mental Illness. Geneva: WHO.

CHAPTER 8

AGREEING LOCAL TARGETS

AGREEING LOCAL TARGETS

Agreeing local targets

8.1 NHS and SSD managers will want to set challenging but realistic targets to monitor their progress towards the Health of the Nation targets. This is particularly important when agreeing targets with alliance partners (see Chapter 5). Targets should therefore be:

- Specific
- Measurable
- Attainable
- Resourced
- Timebound.

8.2 SSDs, DHAs, FHSAs and provider units will all wish to set targets. Managers will wish to agree locally targets to meet local needs and priorities. FHSAs should ensure that GPFHs state in their business and purchasing Plans how they intend to tackle mental illness. This would include, for example, GPFHs' proposed referrals, contract arrangements, use of voluntary services; and arrangements for counselling.

Setting local targets - some examples

8.3 The examples given below suggest some of the areas in which managers may wish to set their own targets. They will also wish to agree similar targets with alliance partners to meet the objectives suggested in Chapter 5.

- To draw up a socio-demographic profile by . . . and to update on an [annual] basis

- To draw up a profile of service provision by . . .

- Full implementation of the CPA by . . .

- Full integration of supervision registers with mental health information systems by . . .

- The computerisation of information collection and dissemination in

  50% of DHAs by . . .

  100% of DHAs by . . .

- Establishing the number of people with severe mental illness in contact with specialist services by . . .

- Minimum dataset (including ethnicity and named key-worker) by . . .

- To reduce vacancies for consultant psychiatrists/occupational therapists/clinical psychologists from . . . % to . . . % by . . .

- To reduce vacancies for approved social workers from . . . % to . . . % by . . .

- To establish effective mechanisms for integrating CPA and care management by . . .

- Reduce numbers of detentions under the Mental Health Act for people from black and other ethnic minority groups by 50% by . . .

- To increase detection rate of depression in General and Social Work practice (assessed by use of local sampling techniques) to . . . % by . .

- To have an equal opportunities policy covering recruitment and service provision, with a system for monitoring it, in place by . . .

Suicide targets

8.4 Suicide numbers are small when measured on a local basis. In setting suicide targets, managers should therefore be wary of attaching too much significance to minor fluctuations in seasonal or annual figures as opposed to comparisons over five year periods.

8.5 Targets can usefully be set for implementing specific measures to reduce suicide risk, for example:

- Establish multi-disciplinary audit meetings by . . .

- To implement observation policies in all units by . . .

- Establish the District/Local Authority rate of suicide for people with severe mental illness by . . .

- Establish regular training sessions for health and social care professionals on assessment and management of suicidal risk by . . .

- To stabilise suicide rate in males (16-44) by . . .

Benzodiazepines

8.6   FHSAs may wish to discuss with GPs agreeing local targets for reductions in benzodiazepine prescriptions. However, the emphasis in any targets should remain on the implementation of appropriate management strategies to deal with the underlying conditions, to replace the use of benzodiazepines.

References
JENKINS, R. (1990) Towards a system of outcome indicators for mental health care. *British Journal of Psychiatry,* **157,** 500-514.
THORNICROFT, G. & STRATHDEE, G. (1991) Mental Health. *British Medical Journal* **303,** 410-2.
MENTAL HEALTH FOUNDATION (1993). *Guidelines for the Prevention and Treatment of Benzodiazepine Dependence.*
NHSME (1993) The Health of the Nation. Local target setting. A discussion paper. Leeds: NHSME.

CHAPTER 9

AGREEING STRATEGIES FOR ACHIEVING LOCAL TARGETS

AGREEING STRATEGIES FOR ACHIEVING LOCAL TARGETS

> **Action summary**
>
> **Regions/Regional offices**
>
> ▌ Ensure that purchasers contract for a comprehensive range of mental health services, delivered through the Care Programme Approach (CPA).
>
> **DHAs, FHSAs and SSDs**
>
> ▌ Develop joint community care plan for commissioning and providing mental health services including appropriate strategies to integrate the CPA and care management.
>
> ▌ Agree action plans across alliances.

The need for a mental health strategy

9.1 The delivery of services to people with mental illness is undergoing a rapid shift with the decommissioning of outdated institutions. A planned approach to this change is necessary to ensure that comprehensive locally-based services able to offer a high quality of care are in place **before** any closure. Plans will need to reflect the results of population and resource profiles and local needs assessment exercises.

Implementing a mental health strategy

9.2 A strategy for service development in mental illness will need to cover a number of components, including:

- information technology (see chapter 11)
- a planned approach to developing a range of community mental health services (see table in section 6.8)
- an assessment of recruitment, training and support needs against current resources (see chapter 10).

9.3 Purchasing authorities can seek detailed advice on establishing and implementing strategic plans in mental health from the Health Advisory Service and the Mental Health Task Force. Further information is at Appendix 9.1.

9.4   DHAs, FHSAs and SSDs will need to develop their own strategies to:

- target resources effectively to meet the needs of the most severely mentally ill people in their resident population (see chapter 7)

- meet gaps in provision, such as in respite care, advocacy, and psychotherapy and counselling services

- identify potential providers of services, including provision from the independent sector.

9.5   It is particularly important that health and social services agencies have agreed clear procedures to ensure that individuals' needs are met at the interface of health and social care.

9.6   The implementation of the Children Act 1989 is having fundamental effects on the purchasing and providing of mental health services for those under 18 years of age. In developing joint strategies NHS providers and SSDs need to consider carefully how to meet the objectives of the Act in relation to child and adolescent mental health services, and services for children with special mental health needs.

9.7   Similar shared responsibilities exist under the Mental Health Act 1983. Appendix 9.2 outlines the respective responsibilities.

The Care Programme Approach

9.8   The Care Programme Approach was introduced in the NHS in April 1991. Provider units are required to initiate, in collaboration with local social services departments, explicit individually-tailored care programmes for all inpatients about to be discharged from mental illness hospitals, and for all new patients accepted by the specialist psychiatric services.

9.9   The Care Programme Approach is designed primarily to improve delivery of care to people with severe mental illness. However, to ensure that they do not 'slip through the safety-net of care', the approach applies to:

a.   **all** people accepted by specialist psychiatric services

b.   **all** psychiatric patients considered for discharge from hospital.

This ensures that all patients are assessed and that no one who might be vulnerable is missed.

The Tiered CPA

9.10 The requirement that the CPA is applied to all patients in contact with the specialist psychiatric services does not mean that all the multi-disciplinary team will need to be involved with every patient. There are in fact several possible levels of CPA, depending upon the severity of the patient's condition. Services should apply the requirements of the CPA sensitively, to ensure that the full multi-disciplinary CPA is applied only to those patients who need it. All other patients in contact with the specialist services should still receive the basic elements of the CPA, but they will not need the same input of staff time. The 'tiered CPA' is discussed further in appendix 9.3, which deals with the CPA.

Supervision Registers (HSG(94)5)

9.11 The CPA has recently been strengthened by the introduction of supervision registers (see also 11.7 and Appendix 11.2 below). The aim of the new registers is to ensure that all those patients diagnosed as suffering from a severe mental illness who are considered to be at significant risk of suicide, severe self-neglect, or of seriously harming other people, are given the priority for the care and follow up that they need. The numbers of such patients are likely to be small.

9.12 The decision whether or not to place a patient on a local supervision register should be taken as part and parcel of the overall care programming process. The information held about an individual on a register is part of his or her health record; the usual rules on confidentiality, and the patient's right to a second clinical opinion, apply. The Department of Health will be publishing further guidance on supervision registers in due course, as part of a guide to inter-agency working for the care and protection of severely mentally ill people.

The Care Programme Approach and Care Management

9.13 Care management is founded on the same principles as the Care Programme Approach, namely that:

- people's needs should be assessed.

- a care plan should then be agreed

- that care plan should be implemented, monitored and reviewed.

9.14 For people subject to the CPA the key worker and care management functions are essentially the same. Both involve coordinating the delivery of an agreed care plan. One way of looking at the CPA is as a specialist variant of care management for people with mental health problems, and the two systems should be capable of being fully integrated with one another.

9.15 Care management can be implemented in various ways. In some areas, care management is viewed as a process in which all staff are involved, and there are no designated care manager posts as such. In others, there are nominated care managers, who may or may not be front-line workers, and who may or may not have their own delegated budgets to purchase services.

9.16 As with the CPA, care management has to be applied in a discriminating way. People with different levels and types of needs need differing levels of continuing involvement by professionals in a coordinating role. One way of doing this is to appoint specific "care managers" only for certain people. For other people, different aspects of the care management function may be shared between different workers as appropriate.

9.17 At present it is most common for care management to be located in social services departments and to be concerned primarily with arranging and coordinating social care services. However, all care management systems should include arrangements for liaison with other agencies in order to ensure the delivery of a coordinated care plan. In well-integrated systems, it is quite possible for the care management function to extend in whole or part to health services as well, and for health professionals to be designated as care managers.

9.18 Although some models are likely to be more effective than others, **any** model of care management can – and should – be integrated with the CPA. The key to integration lies in defining respective responsibilities as clearly as possible, to avoid any possible overlaps or duplications.

9.19 At a minimum local arrangements should ensure that:

- there is a **single** care plan for each person agreed between all the agencies which will be involved in its delivery

- there is a single CPA **key worker** for each person – who carries the full responsibilities of the role and is able to carry them out

- everyone involved in the care plan knows who the key worker is.

9.20 Those performing the CPA key worker role and those undertaking care management responsibilities are performing essentially the same function. Because authorities differ in their use of terminology and their definition of responsibilities, it will not always be the case that a "key worker" is also called a "care manager". However, authorities should be aiming for a situation in which the appointed key worker carries out the care management function of coordinating, monitoring and reviewing the agreed care plan. The selection of the practitioner to fulfil this role should be based on the complexity and volatility of the person's needs, the level of risk, and the balance of health and social care.

9.21 Properly implementing the Care Programme Approach and care management will require the key worker/care manager to have the ability to coordinate services in other disciplines and other agencies, so the process of selecting the practitioner for the role must enjoy cross-agency support. This does not mean that the key worker/care manager must have delegated authority to access directly other agencies' resources, nor that the key worker must be in a position to anticipate or second guess decisions that rightly and legally fall to others. What is required is an agreed scheme of responsibilities, so that, on the one hand, key workers know the limits within which their authority operates, and on the other, that there are protocols that govern the way in which other professionals and agencies will respond to requests from the key worker for modifications to their contribution to the agreed care plan. Authorities and professionals remain individually responsible for the services they contribute to care plans, even though responsibility for overall coordination may lie elsewhere.

9.22 Most people subject to the CPA are likely to require supportive counselling to some degree. Key workers and care managers are likely to provide some of this as a normal part of coordinating people's care plans, and acting as their first point of contact.

9.23 As well as coordinating the care plan, key workers/care managers may also provide an element of the plan in their own right. Where key worker/care managers directly provide part of the care plan, it is essential that they distinguish between the roles and look critically at the total service provision, and dispassionately at their own role within that. The provider role should not be allowed to dominate the coordinating and managing roles, nor *vice versa*.

References

BARNES D. & PHILLIPSON J. (1994) Community care monitoring. Special Study: Mental Health. Heywood: DH.

BOUGHTON M. & DIVALL P. (1994) Care programme approach: the experience in Bath. *Psychiatric Bulletin,* **18(2),** 77-79.

DEPARTMENT OF HEALTH (1990) The care programme approach for people with a mental illness referred to the specialist psychiatric services. (HC(90)23)/LASSL(90)11. Heywood: DH.

DEPARTMENT OF HEALTH (1994) Introduction of supervision registers for mentally ill people from 1 April 1994 (HSG(94)5). Heywood: DH.

DEPARTMENT OF HEALTH SOCIAL SERVICES INSPECTORATE (1991) Assessment systems and care management. London: DH.

DEPARTMENT OF HEALTH SOCIAL SERVICES INSPECTORATE (1992) Care management and assessment: Practice Guidance: Managers' Guide. London: HMSO.

DEPARTMENT OF HEALTH SOCIAL SERVICES INSPECTORATE (1994) Community Care Monitoring First Impressions April to September 1993. London: DH.

KINGDON, D. (1994) The care programme approach. *Psychiatric Bulletin,* **18(2),** 68-70.

ROYAL COLLEGE OF PSYCHIATRISTS (1991) Good medical practice in the aftercare of potentially violent or vulnerable patients discharged from in patient psychiatric treatment. London: RCPsych.

RYAN, P. & FORD, R. (1991) Case management and Community Care. London: RDP.

SCHNEIDER J. *et al.* (1993) Care programming in mental health: a study of implementation and costs in three health districts. Discussion paper 922/2 Personal Social Services Research Unit, Univ. of Kent at Canterbury.

SOCIAL & COMMUNITY PLANNING RESEARCH. (1993) Factors influencing the implementation of the Care Programme Approach. London: HMSO.

SOURCES OF STRATEGIC ADVICE FOR MANAGERS

A.   THE NHS HEALTH ADVISORY SERVICE

I.   The Health Advisory Service (HAS), created in 1969, is an independent body sponsored by the Department of Health. The Director of the HAS reports to the Secretary of State for Health, and Wales. The HAS advises government Ministers (England and Wales only) and the NHS on maintaining and developing high quality services, mainly for elderly and mentally ill people. In 1992 Ministers gave the HAS explicit responsibilities for advising on purchasing.

2.   The HAS conducts its business through:

- thematic reviews – these aim to develop purchasing skills and the quality of local services through the dissemination of advice and good practice.

- Ministerial reviews – reviews of local services are undertaken at the specific request of Ministers, with the aim of identifying problems in service strategy and delivery, and of providing solutions.

- Specialist review services – the Drug Advisory Service reviews services for substance misusers and advises purchasers and providers in around 14 districts a year. The HAS also provides other specialist advisory services for local purchasers and providers.

- Review and Consultancy Service – this service aims to help health authorities develop their skills in purchasing and monitoring providers.

The HAS carries out its work by recruiting, on short-term secondment, leading edge managers and practitioners from a wide variety of professions.

Director: Dr Richard Williams

Address: Health Advisory Service
                       Sutherland House
                       29-37 Brighton Road
                       Sutton
                       Surrey SM2 5AN

Telephone: 081-642-6421

B. THE MENTAL HEALTH TASK FORCE

1. The Mental Health Task Force was created in January 1993 with a two year remit to facilitate the transfer of mental health services away from obsolete hospitals to a balanced range of locally-based services.

2. In its first year the Task Force has commissioned or completed:

   - a study of the remaining large mental hospitals and their plans for closure, with a database which will allow future progress with closures to be monitored

   - the launch of two newsletters: "The Water Tower" (for managers who are involved in the process of closing a long-stay psychiatric hospital) and "Grassroots" (for anyone interested in mental health)

   - a detailed survey of services in three regions

   - the encouragement of good practice through awards of up to £25,000, and a series of good practice videos on ways of meeting needs

   - a series of ten regional conferences for service users and managers, six regional conferences for black and minority groups, and a training programme for users in planning and advocacy.

3. In 1994 the Task Force will:

   - publish booklets on managing transitional costs, good practice in closure programmes, the qualities service elements should possess, and the experience of carers

   - introduce a detailed management and monitoring system for hospital replacement

   - issue further newsletters, including one for local authorities, and complete the series of good practice videos

   - introduce a system to provide comparative data on services, district to district

   - hold a series of regional stakeholder meetings

- culminate its work with users and black people with two major national conferences, and publication of a "Users Charter", a code of practice on advocacy and a book on race and mental health.

4. The Task Force Leader has visited many services and has offered informal advice where appropriate. He will continue to do this and welcomes invitations from purchasers or providers.

Leader: David King

Contact: Alan Bell

Address: Room 235
                Richmond House
                79 Whitehall
                London SWlA 2NS

Telephone: 071-210 5398

RESPONSIBILITIES UNDER THE MENTAL HEALTH ACT

The Code of Practice of the Mental Health Act, revised in 1993, specifies that local agreements should be drawn up in a range of circumstances (see table)

Para. of Code	Policy requirement under Code of of Practice	Responsibility of:		
		H.A.	L.A.	Police
2.11c	Issue guidance to Approved Social Workers (ASWs) about interpreters.		●	
2.14	Issue practical guidance to ASWs on procedures re. displacement of nearest relative (s.29)		●	
2.33	Issue guidance to ASWs re request(s) from nearest relative for ASW assessment (s.13.4).		●	
2.35	Ensure ASWs and doctors receive guidance on use of professional interpreters.	●	●	
10.1	Establish joint policy re. police power to remove person to place of safety (s.136).	●	●	●
10.19	Issue guidance to ASWs on powers of entry (s.135).		●	
11.3	Produce policy with Ambulance Service on conveyance of patients to hospitals.	●	Take lead	●
13.6	Prepare and publish policy on Guardianship (s.7).		●	
14.6	Hospital Managers' policy on providing information to patients.	●		
16.33	Hospital Managers' "Second Opinion Appointed Doctor" system.	●		
18.13	Policy on the use of restraint.	●		
18.16	Policy on the use of seclusion.	●		
18.27	Policy on the use of locked doors on "open" wards.	●		
18.29	Policy on the use of locked doors and secure areas.	●		
19.2	Policy re. behaviour modification programmes.	●		
19.10	Policy on the use of "time-out".	●		
21.2	Policy on procedure re. patients absent without leave (s.18).	●		
24.15	Managers of Special Hospitals policy on witholding mail.	SHSA		
25.1	Policy on searching of patients and their belongings.	●		
27.3	To agree procedures for aftercare with local voluntary organisations (s.117).	●	●	

Appendix 9.3

CARE PROGRAMME APPROACH

Questions about practical application:

1. What is the 'tiered CPA'?

Not all patients will need a multi-disciplinary assessment, care plan and review. Indeed, patients can be divided into three groups, depending upon the severity of their illness, and the level of professional intervention they need:

Minimal CPA. If a patient needs the attention of one member of the team, the CPA requirements are very simple:

- **assessment** – the consultant will probably do the assessment, perhaps with some input from a social worker and mental health nurse;

- **key worker** – the member of the team who will be carrying out care interventions will be the key worker;

- **care plan** – this will be very short, merely indicating the regular interventions planned, on which the patient will be consulted.

Any changes in the patient's condition will be monitored by the member of the team carrying out the interventions. He or she will keep other members of the team informed if there are any major changes in the condition of the patient.

More complex CPA. People with severe mental illness who require the multi-disciplinary care of two or three professionals will require a more complex, multi-disciplinary care plan:

- **needs assessment** – several members of the team will need to be present, including (almost certainly) a psychiatrist, social worker and mental health nurse, and the key worker (if different);

- **key worker** – there will need to be a discussion over the identity of the key worker and how he or she should relate to the care manager;

- **care plan** – the plan will be more complex, requiring interventions from several members of the team, who will need to be aware of what their colleagues are doing.

The full, multi-disciplinary CPA. People with severe mental illness, whose complex health and social care needs are such that they may require care management in addition to the Care Programme Approach, will require full multi-disciplinary assessments, care plan and reviews.

2. **Does the Care Programme Approach just apply to those accepted by psychiatrists?**

   No, it applies to "all in-patients considered for discharge and all new patients accepted by the specialist psychiatric services" and so includes all patients referred to mental health professionals, including psychologists, approved social workers and community mental health nurses, where they receive referrals directly.

3. **What about people who were already being seen in the community by members of psychiatric teams, prior to 1 April 1991?**

   Whilst these patients do not fall within the ambit of the circular, good practice dictates that they are included after the Care Programme Approach is operating for the groups identified above.

4. **What does the Care Programme Approach involve?**

   a. Systematic assessment of the health and social care needs of the patient with particular regard as to whether the patient has a severe and enduring (ie chronic) mental illness.

   b. Drawing up of a package of care agreed with members of the multi-disciplinary team, local authority care managers, GPs, service users and their carers.

   c. Nomination of a key worker to keep in close contact with the patient.

   d. Regular review and monitoring of the patient's needs and progress, and of the delivery of the care programme.

5. **How do you decide if someone has a 'severe and enduring mental illness'?**

   For most psychiatrists and mental health workers, this does not usually prove a difficult clinical decision. It is a judgement made on the basis of the severity and duration of symptoms and disability which may lead patients to have severe social problems because of their inability to cope with ordinary living. This inability to cope might necessitate repeated or lengthy hospital admissions or day care attendance, sheltered accommodation, or long-term medication. Repeated requests for assistance from a person and/or her/his carer should alert staff to the possibility of unmet need.

6.   Who can be a key worker?

Any mental health worker can be designated a key worker. A psychiatrist assessing a patient in an outpatient clinic may become the key worker but this would normally be a non-medical role when other team members are involved in the care of a patient. For most patients with severe and enduring mental illness, a social worker or a community mental health nurse would be appropriate, or an occupational therapist.

7.   How should a key worker be nominated?

Procedures for nomination or allocation of key workers in community mental health teams continue to cause concern. Priorities need to be established and allocation made in a way that reflects patient need and ensures that differing professional skills are used to the best effect. The patient should normally be involved in discussions on the allocation of a key worker.

In most teams the person making the initial assessment of a patient referral usually continues as key worker. This generally saves time and ensures maximum continuity of care. It does however make equitable, appropriate and efficient initial allocation of referrals particularly important. This should be the responsibility of suitably trained and experienced team leaders, who can review whether it is appropriate that the initial assessor continues as key worker, and re-allocate the patient if necessary.

Where a patient is about to be discharged from hospital, the allocation of a key worker needs to be made prior to discharge by the multi-disciplinary team. This should take place at a pre-discharge ward round, or review, to which the patient, any carers or any local authority care manager would normally be invited. The General Practitioner needs to be informed about the proposed Care Programme, the identity of the key worker, and how to contact him or her. When a patient discharges him or herself, a team review may not be possible. Nevertheless, consultation with community agencies, including the General Practitioner and Social Services Department, and any carer involved, is desirable.

8. What if agreement cannot be reached on key worker allocation?

If referrals accepted are placed in priority order and allocation is made by team leaders such disagreements should not arise. Differences in allocation and prioritisation policies between agencies may however need to be addressed at local level. There may also be a need to develop procedures to resolve problems when all possible key workers feel overstretched.

9. What are the responsibilities of a key worker?

    a. To use their professional skills collaboratively in assisting patients and maintaining regular contact with them. This should include consultation with carers.

    b. To provide support and care in a positive, assertive manner which is as acceptable to the user/patient as possible.

    c. To act as a consistent point of contact for users, carers, local authority care manager (if not the key worker) and other professionals.

    d. To ensure the user is registered with a GP and then to work in close contact with the primary care health team (PHCT) and other involved professionals.

    e. To be aware of other resources and provide information or refer as appropriate.

    f. To assist in planning and then monitoring the delivery of the agreed care package, record decisions made about it and ensure that it is reviewed at regular intervals.

A Department of Health conference to consider the role and training needs of key workers under the Care Programme Approach was held in March 1994. A training strategy for key workers is being developed in the light of that conference.

10. What extra documentation does the CPA require?

Basic personal details are collected as part of the initial referral process and so it is difficult to conceive of a reason why they should need to be repeated in CPA documentation.

But they do need to be supplemented. Here is an example of a sheet which can be attached to the inside of the medical and other clinical notes:

Is the Carer involved? (Date(s):..)	Yes/No
Is the person subject to after care under Section 117? (Date(s):..)	Yes/No
Have they been considered for inclusion on the supervision register? (Date(s):..)	Yes/No
Are they included on the supervision register? (Date(s):..)	Yes/No

CURRENT COMMUNITY KEY WORKER
Name: Address: Telephone:

[NB: Revise if there is a change in key worker or any of the above circumstances.]

This needs to be kept up to date – and should be completed on initial assessment, even if it just has the name of the person making that assessment prior to another key worker being appointed.

Care plans should be completed at initial assessments and updated at reviews. This simply means that the care plan which would normally be completed at the end of an assessment and re-assessment, for example in an outpatient clinic or at a review meeting, should be written in the clinical notes. Here is an example of a care plan form:

CARE PROGRAMME APPROACH		
CARE PLAN		
No.	Action.	Worker responsible.

Care plan agreed by:
Patient/user: ....
Key worker: ....
Carer (where relevant): ....

Date: ....
Next review: ....

11. What should a review consist of?

a. Where a patient needs more than a minimal CPA (see above) a review meeting will usually need to be convened. These are however very costly in professional time and so need to be brief with clear agendas. It may be appropriate to review a small group of patients/users who are involved with the same group of professionals at review meetings on the same day.

b. Where a patient needs only a minimal CPA (ie, only one or two workers are involved), a specific review needs to take place and be documented with consideration given to involvement of other professionals and services. However, a review meeting as such may not be necessary.

12. How regularly should reviews occur?

This needs to be determined at the time of key worker allocation and thenceforth at each review. Provision needs to be made for convening reviews rapidly if circumstances warrant it. Where change is occurring or potential problems are foreseen, reviews will need to be more regular, but there is benefit in scheduling reviews of those whose situation is stable at six monthly intervals. This ensures a regular review, and a familiar face and contact point if relapse occurs or situations change.

13. How should the Primary Health Care Team (PHCT) be involved in the CPA?

a. The exchange of information between professionals, with the informed consent of the user/patient is fundamental, not only prior to discharge from hospital or a care episode, but also at regular intervals thereafter. Mental health professionals need to accustom themselves to the concept of referring patients back to primary care.

b. The PHCT and the mental health team should agree the division of clinical responsibilities (eg for physical health checks, the provision of specific treatments or medication supplies, and follow-up arrangements). Where users/patients move between districts, it is essential that respective CMHTs (Community Mental Health Teams) and PHCTs liaise, to ensure that patients are not lost to the specialist and primary care services.

c. PHCTs need to consider the social care needs of their patients in collaboration with the SSD and its care managers.

d. The PHCT and CMHT need to agree and disseminate mechanisms for routine and emergency contact.

e. The PHCT should receive a copy of the care plan.

14. What if a patient discharges him/herself from hospital or is at risk of so doing?

a. Carers, the patient's General Practitioner, and key worker, if already nominated, and any care manager need to be informed immediately. Where the patient specifically forbids contact with the carer they can nevertheless be contacted if they are deemed to be at risk from the patient. In virtually all circumstances attempts should be made to persuade the patient of the benefit of such contact being made.

b. The patient should be offered follow-up care, either in his or her own home, or at an outpatient clinic.

c. A key worker should be nominated to try and contact patients who discharge themselves. Occasionally she or he may have to visit even when a patient has refused follow-up. Although the patient retains the right to refuse to see the key worker, subject to statutory provisions, it is worth persevering: contact can sometimes be re-established at a later stage.

d. There should also be consultation with any social worker involved with patients' families (eg in relation to children in the family).

15. What if a patient refuses contact?

a. Where this occurs a multi-disciplinary discussion (although not necessarily a meeting) may establish alternative ways of presenting a care plan which is acceptable to the patient. The patient may opt only to accept a part of the programme offered and as far as possible, the programme should be sufficiently flexible to accommodate this.

b. Even if the programme is wholly rejected, the team should offer to keep in contact on a regular basis, in consultation with the patient's GP.

c. The carer also should be offered assistance on a regular basis, and a reliable point of contact.

16. Will a patient always require the CPA?

By no means – if a patient's condition improves to such an extent that he or she no longer needs the care of the specialist psychiatric services, then she or he will no longer require a care programme. However patients should not be discharged simply because contact is lost or progress is not being made. Where someone discharges themselves from psychiatric care, the same action as when they discharge themselves from hospital should apply, as above.

17. What if the arrangements for the CPA are not working?

Systems usually have 'teething problems' and so need to be formally reviewed at intervals in the relevant fora, including medical and multi-disciplinary staff meetings.

CHAPTER 10

DEVELOPING HUMAN SKILLS AND RESOURCES

DEVELOPING HUMAN SKILLS AND RESOURCES

Action summary

Directors of SSDs

- Review provision of specialist mental health workers.

DHAs, FHSAs and Directors of SSDs

- Promote, via contracts, multi-disciplinary team working and audit of health and social care.

FHSAs

- Work with NHS provider units and SSDs to develop and support joint training for primary health care teams.

NHS Providers and Managers of SSDs

- Review provision of specialist mental health workers and develop multi-disciplinary team working.

- Assess training needs and opportunities and establish training programmes as necessary.

Staff development

10.1 The primary resource available to managers is the staff who will be implementing programmes to achieve the Health of the Nation targets. Staff will need to be developed to meet their own personal aspirations and to maximise their contribution.

10.2 A number of managers in health and social services and other professional staff have been involved in developing locally-based services to replace mental hospitals, and in implementing change in other areas. They represent an invaluable resource for others, in information, inspiration and training.

10.3 In order to provide efficient health and social care in increasingly community-based services, DHAs and SSDs will want to deploy the right number of trained staff – including psychiatrists, psychologists, community mental health nurses and social workers – to meet most effectively the needs of their local populations. In order to maintain the effectiveness of the workforce it will be important to identify appropriate supervision and support arrangements for staff.

10.4 SSDs will also need to consider the balance of workers between specialist and generic teams, the numbers of ASWs, and how they relate to care managers.

10.5 Managers will need to take account of the availability of staff when moving towards community care; the balance of staff between specialisms; and the availability and training of support workers.

10.6 The following table gives an example of a professional staff profile, relating staff to population base. Targets can be set in ratios of staff to population, and in numbers of vacancies etc. Action should be taken to address any shortfalls in staff numbers identified.

	Total	Rate per 100,000 Population	Vacancies
Consultant Psychiatrists:			
Mental illness			
Forensic			
Old age			
Psychotherapy			
Child and Adolescent			
General Practitioners with further training or qualifications in mental health:			
Clinical psychologists:			
Therapists:			
Occupational therapists			
Physiotherapists			
Art and drama therapists			
Psychiatric Nursing Staff:			
Total (qualified)			
CPNs			
Social workers:			
Specialist mental illness			
Approved social workers			

10.7 Training for all **non-specialist** staff – primary health care teams, social workers, residential, day and home care staff, midwives, casualty staff and hospital and community doctors and nurses – is critical to:

- a better understanding of the needs of users and carers

- the effective management of risks and illnesses

- the improved recognition and assessment of suicidal risk, depression and anxiety.

10.8 A number of steps can be taken to implement effective training for staff:

- identify mental health skills requirements for individual staff groups and audit individual staff members' training needs

- identify requirements for training in multi-disciplinary working and key working skills

- identify staff, users and carers who have such skills to share, and any gaps in trainer availability

- commission external training as appropriate. Consider using voluntary and user organisations, and relevant modules of existing Approved Social Worker (ASW) courses

- liaise between secondary care providers and primary care to provide training opportunities

- ensure quality control with, for example, regular user feedback.

10.9 Providers may wish to concentrate staff development in particular on the implementation of the Care Programme Approach and Care Management. Provider units may wish to run seminars – for the NHS, LA, voluntary groups, users and carers – to ensure staff are aware of their responsibilities and are given the tools to develop effective local implementation strategies. SSDs may wish to run seminars on community care issues for local authority housing staff, NHS staff, voluntary groups and users.

10.10 All professional groups would benefit from the development of general and specialist skills in:

- appropriate care and treatment of postnatal mental illness, eating disorders and pre-senile dementias

- counselling techniques

- behavioural, cognitive and family therapies

- equal opportunities – particularly for women and ethnic minority users of services

- multi-disciplinary and key working

- communication and presentation skills

- management of violent, and potentially violent incidents.

10.11 Joint training between different staff groups and across health and social services will enhance inter-professional collaboration and team working to the benefit of service users and staff.

10.12 Training in assessing suicidal risk needs to be made widely available to staff in areas where contact with suicidal patients regularly occurs. This will include staff in accident and emergency departments and general medical wards; SSD social workers; and members of emergency duty teams in addition to DHA and SSD mental health professionals.

Primary care

10.13 A substantial amount of mental illness is undetected in primary care, leading to inappropriate treatment or referral. 40% of people who commit suicide consult their GP in the previous week. Training and further education for all staff who work in primary health care – GPs, practice nurses, health visitors, district nurses, and midwives – in the recognition and effective treatment of depression, and the assessment and management of suicide risk, could help:

- reduce suicide rates

- increase appropriate referrals to social workers and other sources of social support

- promote the graded replacement of benzodiazepines with non-prescribing interventions.

10.14 The Defeat Depression campaign has developed training packages for use in general practice. Similar packages could be developed locally for recognition and management of other mental disorders.

10.15 A senior GP fellow at the Royal College of General Practitioners has been appointed to take a national lead in continuing GP education in mental illness, with the task of promoting the education of the primary health care team in this area and cascading information through Regional Advisors in General Practice. Regional Advisors are well placed to co-ordinate the development of training in mental illness for GPs as part of their continuing medical education.

10.16 Research is in progress into:

- the use of a GP facilitator in mental health education

- the use of practice nurses in the management of depression

- developing an optimal whole practice approach to mental health care.

10.17 FHSAs may wish to encourage GPs to consider how best to integrate their work with the specialist psychiatric services. PHCTs might wish to employ additional practice nurses and counselling support staff. It is essential that these staff are appropriately trained, maintain close links with the secondary services, and are involved in multi-disciplinary audit. In addition, FHSAs and GPs might wish to discuss with directors of social services about how they can best obtain social work advice or social work sessions in GP surgeries or health centres.

Clinical psychologists

10.18 The longstanding shortage of clinical psychologists across the country needs to be addressed. In order to meet current demand for specialised services, providers will need to develop guidelines for the prioritization of referrals and a consultancy model of working (as advocated by the Manpower Planning Advisory Group, see references).

Social workers

10.19 A minimum of 50% of all people on social workers caseloads, irrespective of whether individuals are accepted by the mental health services, other specialist (eg elderly, children) or generic teams, have a mental illness.

10.20 Other than when local circumstances dictate, evidence suggests that attaching social workers to mental health rather than area-based teams leads to the provision of better mental health care. Specialist social workers in Child and Adolescent Mental Health services (CAMHs) may facilitate better liaison between SSD children's services and the CAMHs.

10.21 Directors of social services need to consider carefully how best to deploy ASWs to ensure that they are available for statutory mental health work, and are accessible to other social work and local authority colleagues to provide advice on mental health issues. Directors should also seriously consider allocating specific mental health responsibilities to senior management posts in planning and service provision, in order to preserve the focus on mental illness within the organisation.

10.22 All social workers – including those working in non-specialist mental health settings – would benefit from basic or further training in:

- recognition of mental health problems, including assessment of suicide risk

- steps to help people with mental illness, including appropriate referral for specialist clinical opinion and treatment

- an understanding of the criminal justice system.

Occupational and other therapists

10.23 Staff trained in the provision of therapy services are generally in short supply. The main therapists working in the treatment of mental illness are:

Occupational therapists	developing skills of independent living.
Art, music, drama therapists	working in psychotherapies.
Speech therapists	developing speech and communication skills for relationship building.
Physiotherapists	influencing psychological health through physical approaches such as the use of relaxation, exercise and the management of disabilities.

Dieticians   giving dietary advice to people suffering
                                      from eating disorders, dietary neglect, or
                                      who are long-stay patients about to
                                      leave hospital.

Psychiatrists

10.24 Shortages are progressively but slowly being addressed as part of central personnel planning.

Nursing staff

10.25 All nurses, midwives and health visitors have a role to play in contributing to the achievement of the mental illness targets. It is vital that they receive appropriate education and training to enable them to make that contribution. The Common Foundation Programme of Project 2000 should give pre-registration students a better understanding of psychological needs and problems. Further post-registration programmes will need to be developed for qualified staff, for example, in dealing with mothers with young children.

10.26 The registered mental health nurse is the specialist nurse who is educated and trained to provide care and treatment for people with mental illness, and to contribute to prevention and health promotion. Mental health nursing has undergone radical changes over recent years. As a result, the Secretary of State for Health instituted a review of Mental Health Nursing. The report of the review was published by HMSO in March 1994, entitled "Working in Partnership – A Collaborative Approach to Care"; it makes recommendations across the whole range of mental health nursing practice.

Multi-disciplinary team working

10.27 The integrated delivery of services to meet the social and health needs of users of mental health services requires a high degree of integrated working between staff. Each member of a multi-disciplinary team brings specific skills, although there will be overlap, particularly in relation to psychological management. A multi-disciplinary team will normally consist of:

- a nurse

- a psychiatrist

- a social worker

- an occupational therapist

- a psychologist.

10.28 Crisis intervention teams usually include a psychiatrist approved under Section 12 of the Mental Health Act 1983, an approved social worker and a community mental health nurse available on a 24-hour basis for assessment and management of patients. However, all areas must have social workers and psychiatrists approved under the Mental Health Act 1983 readily available on a 24-hour basis to respond to requests for assessment from GPs, police doctors, etc.

Developing audit

10.29 Audit should take place across primary and secondary care, as well as between health and social services, to identify any problems at the interface of service provision. Staff co-operation in multi-disciplinary audit of treatment and care in cases of homicide, suicide or parasuicide will greatly assist in developing good practice.

10.30 Management can facilitate the process of multi-disciplinary audit by ensuring staff have time to meet.

10.31 Suicides of people who are not in touch with specialist mental health teams should be reviewed by the primary health care team wherever possible. Primary care review can be co-ordinated through Medical Audit Advisory Groups, and would benefit from close working with District Medical Audit Committees, the aim being to increase knowledge of suicide and its prevention. If staff from the SSD have been working with the suicide's family, they too should be involved in the audit.

10.32 FHSAs will wish to support reviews of benzodiazepine use and the development of policies to replace their use over time with non-prescribing interventions.

Review of psychotherapy services

10.33 Health Authorities' and fundholding GPs' responsibility to purchase mental health services for their population or patients includes buying psychotherapy services. However, the task of commissioning psychotherapies to contribute to mental health gain of the population is particularly difficult. The Department of Health is therefore reviewing the role of psychotherapy and psychotherapy training in the NHS, examining research evidence for the efficacy of psychotherapeutic interventions for different mental health problems, and collating evidence on ways to improve the quality and cost effectiveness of NHS psychotherapy services. The results of this review will become available to the NHS in 1995.

References

General

NHSTD (1992) Training and User Involvement in Mental Health Services. Bristol: NHSTD.

Primary care

CORNEY, R. H., JENKINS, R. (1992) Counselling in primary care. London: Routledge.

DARLING, C., TYRER, P. (1990) Brief encounters in general practice: liaison in general practice psychiatry clinics. *Psychiatric Bulletin,* **14,** 592-594

DEFEAT DEPRESSION CAMPAIGN (1993) Defeat Depression: management guidelines. London: DH.

GASK, L., BOARDMAN, J. & STANDART, S. (1991) Teaching Communication Skills: A problem based approach. *Postgraduate Education for General Practice* **2,** 7-15

Social work

CCETSW (1993) Requirements and guidance for the training of social workers to be considered for approval in England and Wales under the 1983 Mental Health Act. London: CCETSW.

FISHER, M. *et al* (1984) Mental health social work observed. National Institute Social Services Library No.45.

HUXLEY, P. (1988) Social Work Practice in Mental Health. Aldershot: Gower.

ISSAC, B., MINTY, E.B. & MORRISON, R.M. (1986) Children in care – the association with mental disorder in the parents. *British Journal of Social Work,* **16,** 325-9

DEPARTMENT OF HEALTH SOCIAL SERVICES INSPECTORATE (1991) Approved social workers: developing a service. London: DH SSI.

Nursing

BROOKER, C. (1990) Community Psychiatric Nursing: a Research Perspective. London: Chapman & Hall.

BROOKER, C. & WHITE, E. (1992) Community Psychiatric Nursing: a Research Perspective. Volume 2. London: Chapman & Hail.

DEPARTMENT OF HEALTH/ROYAL COLLEGE OF NURSING (1994) Good Practice in the Administration of Depot Neuroleptics – a Guidance Document for Mental Health and Practice Nurses. London: DH/RCN.

DEPARTMENT OF HEALTH (1994) Working in Partnership – a Collaborative Approach to Care: Report of the Mental Health Nursing Review Team. London: HMSO.

Clinical psychology

DEPARTMENT OF HEALTH MANPOWER PLANNING ADVISORY GROUP (1990) Clinical Psychology Project: Full Report. London: Department of Health.

ROBINSON M.H., FRANCH, R. & BLAND, M. (1984) Clinical psychology in primary care: controlled clinical and economic evaluation. *British Medical Journal,* **288,** 1805-8.

WILCOCK, P. & ROSSITER, R. (June 1990) Clinical Psychology and General Managers. *Health Services Management.* 139-41.

Interprofessional collaboration

FALLOON, I. & LILLIE, F. (April 7 1988) Science in the community. *Health Service Journal* **98 5095**:392.

GOOD PRACTICES IN MENTAL HEALTH/IAMHW (1990) Community mental health teams/centres Information pack. London: GPMH.

KINGDON, D.C. (1992) Interprofessional collaboration in mental health. *Journal of Interprofessional Care,* **6, 2,** 141-8.

WEAVER, F. & PATMORE, C. (1990) United fronts. *Health Service Journal.* **100, 5223**:1554-1555.

Psychiatrists

JENKINS, R. (1994) The Health of the Nation Recent Government Policy and Legislation. *Psychiatric Bulletin* **18,** 324-7.

CHAPTER 11

DEVELOPING INFORMATION RESOURCES

DEVELOPING INFORMATION RESOURCES

Action summary

NHS Purchasers and Directors of SSDs

▪ Agree a plan with relevant providers for the development of mental health information systems.

FHSAs

▪ Assist in improving and standardising mental health data collection within primary care.

NHS Providers and Managers of SSDs

▪ Discuss with mental health teams and service users their requirements for both patient-based and collated information.

▪ Identify management information needs for resource management, quality control and contracting.

▪ Establish compatible information collection (manual & IT) between health and social services.

The need for information

11.1 Information on service provision, service use, population needs and the epidemiology of mental illness has traditionally been sparse and of poor quality. The state of transition of many mental health services, the dispersed nature of modern mental health care, and the tendency of health care information systems to reflect the episodic nature of acute care rather than the caseload management approach of chronic care have all hampered development. Unreliable and irrelevant information has often been collected at great expense, whilst real information needs have been ignored.

11.2 Information is integral to:

● assessing needs

● resource management (including staff management) and planning

● joint working between health and social care professionals

- ensuring the effective delivery of appropriate care to the individual

- measuring the effectiveness of different treatments, and treatment and care settings, for clinical audit and research

- providing the basis for more refined contracting.

11.3 A more coherent and cost effective approach to the collection, dissemination and use of information is therefore essential. This is not only the case within the NHS, but also between health and social services.

11.4 Strategic reviews of information collection are now occurring within mental illness services, including:

- the Public Health Information Strategy – a review of central needs for information

- Community Information Systems for Providers

- Personal Social Services Information Systems Strategy – a review of personal social services data collection.

Principles of information systems

11.5 Successful information systems enhance the ability both of clinicians to treat patients and of managers to manage. The following are key principles which should underpin effective information systems:

i. information and information systems should be structured the way clinicians operate in their care of mentally ill people. Therefore data structures should reflect the fact that many patients, particularly those at greatest risk, will be receiving continuous, as opposed to episodic care. Rather than being either in- or out-patients, at any time they will be receiving a range of types of care from a number of different professionals. Information systems should also reflect needs arising from the geographically dispersed nature of modern mental health care. Ideally, professionals should be able to enter and access data about patients while 'on the move'.

ii. Information systems are effective to the extent that the information is used. The measure of success should be who is using the information and for what purposes rather than how many computers have been installed.

iii. Joint working, both within the NHS and between the NHS and related agencies, is dependent on common coding languages. All computer systems within the NHS should be designed to conform to the coding and technical standards being developed in the NHS Information Management and Technology Strategy. Social services departments should be closely involved in the design and implementation of systems.

iv. Implementation of computer systems is a major task. It requires the close involvement of the most senior managers and clinicians. Appointment of a suitably able information technology manager is crucial.

v. Even the most finely tailored computer system will change some aspects of the way staff work. Local operational policies are always needed to clarify the allocation of relevant tasks and the extent of permitted access to information. These issues should be determined in close consultation with those staff affected at all levels. This will engender a sense of ownership, thereby easing the transition to the new way of working.

vi. Successful introduction of computer systems depends upon a comprehensive training strategy for the staff involved. This should not be limited to training staff how to use the software purchased, but should also include detailed workshops for clinicians and managers to explore how they might get the most use out of new systems. Simple computer-based training in basic keyboard skills should always be available.

vii. Information audit to ensure data security and accuracy is essential. A policy for this should be an integral part of an operational policy for information systems.

viii. The use and disclosure of information is subject to current guidance on the confidentiality of health information, and is also set out in LAC(88)17. Full safeguards should be built into all systems.

Information systems and key policy initiatives.

11.6 Current mental health care policy has two key strands, the Care Programme Approach and *The Health of the Nation*.

The Care Programme Approach

Health Authorities are required to ensure, either directly or through the contracting process, that individuals referred to the psychiatric services or leaving hospital receive the support they need through a framework of regular reviews of their health and social care needs and key worker supervision (see Appendix 9.3 above). Information systems should record the patient's situation at regular reviews and ultimately also routine contacts with the key worker. This will provide the means by which:

- agreed care programmes are crystallised and made available to relevant professionals

- the size and severity of key worker caseloads can be monitored

- patients falling out of care can be identified both to prompt further outreach and as a measure of service performance

- aggregate estimates of the volumes of various types of care required can be produced, enabling providers and purchasers to identify mismatches between need and provision

- regular evidence can be provided for purchasers of progress with implementation of the CPA. An anonymised data set which would permit effective review of a provider units performance is set out as Appendix 11.1

- data can be gathered about the health and social functioning of mentally ill people for Health of the Nation targets and other purposes (see below).

11.7 The Care Programme Approach has been extended recently in the guidance on setting up Supervision Registers (HSG(94)5). This requires all Health Authorities to ensure through the contracting process that provider units:

- set up registers identifying patients who are at significant risk of suicide, of doing serious harm to others, or of serious self-neglect

- consider, at reviews of patients under the Care Programme Approach, whether the patient should be registered. (By 1 October 1994 the status of all existing patients should have been reviewed to determine whether they should be placed on the register

- incorporate the supervision register in the development of mental health information systems to support the full implementation of the Care Programme Approach.

11.8 It is envisaged that existing information systems sufficient to support fully the Care Programme Approach will require only simple modifications to comply with the new requirements. Supervision registers should not be separate from such systems as long as the information described in Appendix 11.2 is recorded and the procedures outlined in the Guidelines are in place.

The Health of the Nation

11.9 The Health of the Nation sets three main targets in relation to mental illness. Two require the gathering of special information.

Target C1 is:

to improve the health and social functioning of mentally ill people.

No current data source provides adequate information to permit an operational definition of this target at present. To meet this requirement, the Department has commissioned the Research Unit of the Royal College of Psychiatrists to develop a brief, 12 item rating scale for use as an integral part of routine Care Programme Reviews. This instrument (called HoNOS) has been piloted widely and is currently undergoing full field trials in 18 provider units. Development will be complete in time for its introduction in the 1996/7 contracting year. A copy of the field trial version is included as Appendix 11.3.

11.10 When implemented, HoNOS will support a wide range of functions in addition to the monitoring of the first Health of the Nation mental illness target. For example:

- clinical caseload management requires standardised measures of caseload severity

- clinical audit requires measures beyond diagnosis which will illuminate variations in outcome between geographic localities or clinical teams

- casemix classification for mental health care requires the type of information in HoNOS in addition to diagnosis to delineate Healthcare Resource Groups (HRGs).

11.11 Department officials have had informal discussions about the IT implications of HoNOS with suppliers of computerised information systems designed to support the Care Programme Approach. The additional data gathering task appears to present no significant problem for any of the systems currently known to the Department. Provider units should ensure that specifications for any new computer systems include the requirements of HoNOS.

11.12 Target C3 is:

> **To reduce the suicide rate of severely mentally ill people by at least 33% by the year 2000 (from the life-time estimate of 15% in 1990 to no more than 10%).**

Measuring this will require central collection of information about both the numbers of relevant deaths and the numbers of severely mentally ill people. Initially, the number of severely mentally ill people will be considered to be the number of individuals who are subject to a Care Programme (as discussed above). Thus mental health information systems must be capable readily of indicating this information.

The link with primary care

11.13 Close working between primary care and specialist services is essential to the provision of seamless care. FHSAs have a key role to play in facilitating this. GPs will be concerned:

- to ensure that specialist services keep in close contact about relevant developments in the care of patients on their lists

- that Health Authority purchasing reflects the pattern of need in the population as a whole.

In addition, fund holding GPs will wish to purchase a range of specialist mental health services for their patients. The planning and implementation of systems should recognise all these requirements.

References
ROYAL COLLEGE OF PSYCHIATRISTS (1992) *Report of Mental Health Services Information Group*. London: RCPsych.
SAYCE, L. (4 July 1991) Registering: A risky business. *Social Work Today, 12–13*.

Appendix 11.1

SUGGESTED DATA SET FOR MONITORING THE IMPLEMENTATION OF MENTAL HEALTH CARE AS SET OUT IN CARING FOR PEOPLE AND THE CARE PROGRAMME APPROACH.

INFORMATION REQUIREMENTS

A minimum data set of information for mental health services is being drawn up as part of the Community Information Systems Project and will be discussed with the NHS in 1994/5. Purchasers and providers seeking in the interim to identify a data set to document current care activity may consider the following list of items as a starting point. All these items which could readily be gathered in most information system of the type discussed, could be recorded for all patients under the CPA during the preceding period on a quarterly or annual basis.

Current age

Sex

Ethnic Group

DHA of normal residence

Main diagnosis (Where suffering from dementia this should take precedence)

HoNOS scores at most recent review

Thus when available, current HRG.

Joiner/leaver status i.e

- Joined in last quarter
- Left in last quarter
- Both joined and left in last quarter
- Neither joined nor left in last quarter

CPA Start date

CPA End date

Date of most recent review

Components of current care programme including type of accommodation.

Discipline of key worker (eg CPN, Social Worker)

Key worker monitoring status. This could have two conditions:

- Monitoring contact overdue
- Monitoring contact not overdue

Whether on Supervision Register

Supervision Register Joiner/Leaver Status

For Supervision Register leavers, reason for leaving – i.e.

- Died

- Transferred

- No longer considered at risk

Category of Supervision

Whether under legal compulsion

Appendix 11.2

SUPERVISION REGISTERS.

The data set required for inclusion on a supervision register as set out in HSG(94)5 is as follows:

Part 1. Identification.

i. Patient's full name, including known aliases, home address including postcode (or 'no fixed address'), sex, and date of birth.

ii. Patient's current legal status in respect of the Mental Health Act (i.e. whether on leave, under Guardianship or subject to section 117 aftercare or supervised discharge, when available).

Part 2. Nature of risk.

i. Category of risk and nature of specific warning indicators.

ii. Evidence of specific episodes of violent or self destructive behaviours (including **relevant** criminal convictions) or severe self neglect.

Part 3. Key worker and relevant professionals.

i. Name and contact details for patient's key worker.

ii. Name and contact details of other professionals involved in the care of the patient including the consultant responsible for the care of the patient.

Part 4. Care Programme.

i. Date of registration

ii. Date of last review

iii. Date of next programmed review

iv. Components of care programme.

Health of the Nation Outcome Scale for Adult Mental Illness: Field Trial Version

Rate 9 if not known or not applicable

I   Problems resulting from aggressive or disruptive behaviour by patient/ client in the past two weeks

√   Includes aggression due to any cause, e.g. drugs, alcohol, psychosis, etc.

0   No problems of this kind during the period rated.

1   Occasional undue irritability, quarrels, etc, but generally calm.

2   Includes: occasional aggressive gestures, pushing or pestering others; persistent threatening verbal aggression; lesser damage to property (e.g. broken cup, window).

3   Physically aggressive to others (short of rating 4); persistently threatening manner; more serious destruction of property.

4   At least one serious physical attack on others or on animals; severely destructive of property (e.g. firesetting); persistent seriously intimidating or obscene behaviour.

2   Suicidal thoughts, non-accidental self-injury

x   Does not include accidental self-injury due e.g. to dementia or severe learning disability.

0   No problem of this kind during the period rated.

1   Occasional/fleeting thoughts about ending it all but little risk; no self-harm.

2   Minor risk during period; includes non-hazardous self-harm e.g. wrist-scratching.

3   Moderate risk of deliberate self-harm; includes preparatory acts e.g. collecting tablets.

4   Serious suicidal attempt and/or deliberate self-injury during period.

3   Health or social problems of patient/client associated with alcohol or drug misuse (illegal use of drugs)

x   Does not include aggressive/destructive behaviour due to alcohol or drugs, rated at Scale 1.

0   No problem of this kind during the period rated.

1   Occasional loss of control of drinking or drug-taking but no serious social problems during the period rated.

2   Frequent loss of control, with some but not serious social or physical harm.

3   Marked dependence on alcohol or drugs with serious work, family or relationship problems; and/or drunk driving etc, etc; and/or physical illness.

4   Incapacitating physical or mental problem due to alcohol or drug misuse.

4   Problems involving memory, orientation, understanding

0   No problem of this kind during the period rated.

1   Non-clinical memory or understanding problems e.g. forgets names occasionally.

2   Mild but definite problems of memory or understanding e.g. has lost way in a familiar place or failed to recognise a familiar person; sometimes mixed up about simple decisions.

3   Marked disorientation of time, place or person, bewildered by everyday events; speech is sometimes incoherent.

4   Severe disorientation, e.g. unable to recognise relatives, at risk of accidents, speech incomprehensible.

5   Problems associated with physical illness or disability

Illness or disability that limits or prevents movement, or impairs sight or hearing, or otherwise interferes with personal functioning.

√   Include side-effects from medication.

0   No significant physical health problem during the period rated.

1   Temporary health problem during the period (e.g. cold, non-serious fall, etc).

2   Physical health problem imposes moderate restriction on mobility.

3   Severe degree of restriction on activity due to physical health problem.

4   Complete incapacity due to physical health problem.

6   Mood disturbance

If both depressed and expansive mood disturbance, rate the most severe.

x   Does not include suicidal ideation or attempts, rated at Scale 2.

x   Does not include aggressive or destructive behaviour due to elated mood, rated at Scale 1.

0   No problems associated with mood disturbance during the period rated.

1   Gloomy; or transient mood changes **associated with life events.**

2   Mild but definite depression and distress: preoccupied with feelings of guilt, loss of self-esteem or sleep/appetite disturbance.

   Alternatively physically and mentally overactive; rapid speech, actions influenced by inflated self-esteem.

3   Physical or mental slowing or agitation, guilt, inappropriate self-blame.

   Alternatively reckless judgement, pressure of speech, severe physical over-activity, denial of tiredness.

4   Severe retardation (stupor at the most severe) or agitation, severe guilt or self-accusation (delusional at the most severe).

   Alternatively may be careless of environmental dangers; impulsive behaviour; constantly changing interests; extravagant plans without reference to reality; disinhibited thoughts and activities (delusional at the most severe) or severe mood swings.

7   Problems associated with hallucinations and delusions

x   Does not include delusions associated with depressed or elated mood, rated at Scale 6.

x   Does not include aggressive or destructive behaviours due to psychotic symptoms, rated at Scale 1.

0   No evidence of hallucinations or delusions during the period rated.

1   Mildly eccentric beliefs not in keeping with cultural norms.

2   Definite preoccupation with delusions or hallucinations (e.g. voices, visions) but little distress to patient or manifestation in bizarre behaviour, i.e. clinically present but mild.

3   Marked preoccupation with delusions or hallucinations, causing much distress and/or manifested in markedly bizarre behaviour, i.e. moderate clinical problem.

4   Mental state is seriously and adversely affected by delusions or hallucinations, causing severe distress to patient/client and/or others.

8 Other mental and behavioural problems

√ Includes all mental and behavioural problems not considered at Scales 1–7: e.g. panics, phobias, obsessions, anorexia, bulimia, sleep problems, fatigue, persistent complaints about bodily symptoms with no known physical cause. This scale covers all these problems and is therefore worded generally. If more than one problem occurred during the period, rate only the problem which you judge to be the most severe.

0 No evidence of any of these problems during period rated.

1 Minor persistent problem, or short-lived problem associated with life events.

2 One or more of the problems listed is clinically present, but there are relatively symptom-free intervals and patient/client has a degree of control, i.e. mild level.

3 Constant preoccupation with problem(s). Occasional severe attack or distress, with loss of control (e.g. has to avoid anxiety provoking situations altogether, call in a neighbour to help, etc) i.e. moderate level of problem.

4 Severe, persistent problem(s) dominates most activities.

9 Problems with making supportive social relationships

√ Includes problems (within family and/or in wider social network) due (a) to active or passive withdrawal from social relationships; or (b) to relationships that provide little or no comfort or support to patient.

x Does not include aggressive disruptive behaviour in relationships, rated at Scale 1.

0 No evidence of significant problems during the period.

1 Either transient or long-lasting mild problems but accepted by patient.

2 Major problems in making supportive relationships but not 3.

3 Persisting major problems due to (a) active or passive withdrawal from social relationships or (b) to relationships that provide little or no comfort or support.

4 Severe social isolation due to inability to communicate socially and/or withdrawal from social relationships.

10   Social environment: housing and locality

Given this individual's problems as **rated at Scales 1–9 above,** is the housing and locality appropriate for promoting the best use of his/her positive capabilities and requirements for a reasonable quality of life.

0   No problems with accommodation: appropriate to needs, affordable, reasonable quality, sufficient shelter needed by this individual. Acceptable (or own choice) locality.

1   Accommodation reasonably appropriate for this individual but mild or transient problems (e.g. not ideal location) but problems not at the level of ratings 2 to 4.

2   Accommodation physically appropriate but associated problems e.g. cost, insecure tenure, unhelpful or intrusive neighbours; or accommodation inappropriate because of e.g. location, poor repair or facilities.

3   Severe and distressing multiple problems with accommodation as above.

4   Roofless, at risk of eviction, or in totally inadequate accommodation.

11   Social environment: employment, recreation, finance

Given this individual's problems as **rated at Scales 1–9 above,** is the social environment appropriate for promoting the best use of his/her positive capabilities and requirements for a reasonable quality of life? Does the absence of any of these prevent the patient/client from functioning at the optimal level achievable? Consider at two levels:

(a)   basic requirements: money, food, clothes, protection from exploitation etc.

(b)   additional requirements: useful occupation, companionship, education, interests, choice.

0   Given this individual's problems **as rated as Scales 1–9 above,** (a) and (b) are in place, allowing achievement of optimal functioning.

1   The basic requirements as listed in (a) are provided for, but additional requirements (b) that could help achieve optimum autonomy for this patient/client are not available.

2   The basic requirements as in (a) are provided for but there are many gaps in additional requirements (b) that could help achieve optimum autonomy for this individual.

3   Only a minimum standard of living, and few options for self-improvement.

4   This individual is below the minimum standard of living level; and/or at serious risk of destitution.

12   Overall severity of functional disability

Taking all previous information into account, make a judgement as to the level of overall disability. Include difficulties in performing any of the Activities of Daily Life. Consider efficient weekly budgeting, living arrangements, occupation (within and outside home), recreation, physical mobility, shopping, use of transport, self-care.

Rate this on a scale of 0-100. As in all the scales, '0' means 'no problem'. You can use any number to represent problems but here are some general guidelines:

0-20 No problems. During period rated, good function in all areas, no need of support.

21-40 Minor problems only.

41-60 Major inability to perform one or more complex skills such as weekly budgeting, occupation, shopping, making travel arrangements.

61-80 Major problems in some areas of self-care (eating, washing, dressing, toilet) as well as major inability to perform several complex skills.

81-100 Severe disability or incapacity in all or nearly all areas of functioning.

CHAPTER 12

ESTABLISHING PURCHASING AND MONITORING ARRANGEMENTS

ESTABLISHING PURCHASING AND MONITORING ARRANGEMENTS

Action summary

All NHS and SSD Managers

▌ Continue to review mechanisms of quality assurance.

▌ Establish joint monitoring mechanisms between NHS and LAs.

▌ Involve voluntary organisations and users/carers in monitoring processes.

Regions/Regional Offices

▌ Monitor DHAs and FHSAs through the performance management process.

FHSAs

▌ Assist and monitor GP fund-holders in developing purchasing plans.

NHS (DHA and GPFH) Purchasers and Directors of SSDs

▌ Develop contracts for a wide range of services, including the CPA, supervision registers and care management, and the provision of continuing care and emergency access (including medical and social work staff approved under the Mental Health Act 1983).

▌ Develop joint purchasing arrangements.

▌ Use contracting process pro-actively to negotiate with existing and potential providers to achieve changes in service provision.

Contracting

12.1 Contracting is a powerful tool with which purchasers of mental health services can shape service provision and implement change.

12.2 Purchasers need to develop a clear vision of service development – based upon a thorough assessment of need, a respect for autonomy and an understanding of the range and suitability of different service settings and treatments. Prospective contracting – drawing up provisional contracts looking forwards over a three to five year period – will draw this vision to the attention of the service by:

- setting a timescale for change and progress

- signalling purchasing intentions to existing and prospective providers, enabling them to put in place mechanisms to meet the planned contracts.

12.3 Contracts should aim to describe what should be delivered without being over-prescriptive about how those service objectives are to be met.

12.4 Purchasers will wish to consider what measures they will need to incorporate in their future contracts, using the proposals outlined in this handbook as guidance. Some of the key areas purchasers will wish to address in their contracts are:

- user involvement – including access to advocates

- the range of services required

- quality standards – including the rights of users

- multi-disciplinary audit of treatment and suicide

- service providers' responsibilities under the Mental Health Act 1983 and Children Act 1989

- arrangements for emergency access to members of mental health teams, including to staff recognised under the Mental Health Act 1983

- the implementation of the CPA, care management and section 117 aftercare, including arrangements for discharge planning

- the provision of services for particular groups – such as the need for continuing care beds and services for mentally disordered offenders. Contracting provides an opportunity to incorporate services for mentally disordered offenders into mainstream services

- monitoring arrangements – including independent monitoring

- clear policies for managing suicidal patients in hospital, including observation policies

- discharge and supervision register policies.

12.5 The following table suggests some of the key considerations purchasers may wish to take into account when seeking to purchase for the needs of particular groups or conditions.

	Examples of purchasing considerations
Homeless people	Requirements for supported accommodation. Specialist teams or workers.
Children and Adolescents	Provision of specialist mental health workers, teams and units. Co-ordination of service delivery between child and adult mental health, generic social services and education services.
Older people	In-patient acute assessment facilities, respite, domiciliary, day care and community services, including access to community mental health nurses.
Black and other ethnic minority groups	Issues of access and acceptability. Interpreting and advocacy services.
Women	Choice of female key worker/therapist. Single sex areas in units.
Mentally disordered offenders	Integration with mainstream services. Court diversion schemes and local secure units.
People with learning disability and mental illness	Co-ordination of service delivery between child and adult mental health and specialist learning disability services.
People with eating disorders	Access to specialist in-patient facilities on sub-Regional basis. Availability of family and cognitive therapy.
People with puerperal disorders	In-patient facility – local, but need for appropriately trained and experienced staff may necessitate tertiary referral.
Liaison psychiatry	Defining responsibility in contracts with provider units.
Physical and mental illness	Definition of responsibility for liaison psychiatry services in contracts with provider units.
Pre-senile dementias, brain damage	Advantages of local provision balanced against development of more specialist but sub-regional units.

12.6 The Mental Health Act Commission has developed guidance on contracting for Mental Health Act services (described in its Fifth Biennial Report).

Joint purchasing

12.7 Joint purchasing offers a mechanism through which health and social services resources for mental health can be allocated very effectively. It may be appropriate for Joint Consultative Committees to have oversight of this process. Joint purchasing will help:

- the development of a seamless service

- ensure the most appropriate delivery of care

- increase interprofessional co-operation

- eliminate the duplication of resources.

12.8 The cultural differences between the NHS and SSDs should not be underestimated. Perseverance may be needed in negotiating a mode of working acceptable to both organisations. In moving towards joint purchasing, DHAs, FHSAs, GPFHs and SSDs will wish to consider:

- drawing up an agreed strategy and plan, including timetable, for full implementation of joint purchasing, ensuring that a full range of services is available during the period of transition

- identifying specific areas – such as staffed residential accommodation for people with mental illness, or day care etc – for initial joint purchasing. Joint Care Planning Teams can be useful in developing and defining areas to be covered

- establishing jointly staffed community teams in each locality and better systems of joint work between social workers, community mental health nurses, GPs and other members of primary health care teams

- transferring resources with patients as they move from long-stay hospitals to social service settings.

Monitoring progress

12.9 Monitoring is integral to good management. Monitoring will assist in:

- assessing progress towards local and national targets

- identifying any inhibitors in making progress towards targets and facilitating early and effective management action

- ensuring that service users do not fall through the net of care at the interface between health and social services agencies

- ensuring that equal opportunities in service provision are effectively applied, for example by having a named person in the purchasing authority to monitor equal opportunities practice in providers.

12.10 Particular aspects of monitoring which managers at both purchaser and provider level will want to consider include:

- monitoring both quantity and quality aspects of service provision

- monitoring patients' rights – particularly where people are detained under the Mental Health Act 1983

- joint monitoring between the NHS and SSDs.

12.11 Effective monitoring of services can be enhanced by the inclusion of monitors independent of the specialist health or social services, particularly organisations representing or controlled by users. They may be especially helpful in monitoring quality standards, such as accessibility and information provision, and in identifying gaps in services which may otherwise go unnoticed. Monitors may include:

- Community Health Councils

- voluntary organisations

- advocacy workers

- user groups

- primary care workers.

12.12 Purchasers and providers can support them in this role by:

- making full information in clear language available

- ensuring rights of access to premises and appropriate management meetings

- providing adequate funding.

The Report of the Inquiry into the Care and Treatment of Christopher Clunis recommended that statutory bodies and voluntary agencies working in the mental health field recruit, train and support members of the public who wish to be 'befrienders' of patients subject to section 117 aftercare (45.4). Providers may wish to take this idea forward, both for section 117 patients, and for other users.

Regional role in monitoring

12.13 Regions/Regional Offices will need to monitor DHAs through the performance management process. They can call upon the Health Advisory Service to assist in monitoring good practice (see Appendix 9.1).

Central monitoring

12.14 The NHS Executive (NHS E), Regions/Regional Offices and the Social Services Inspectorate (SSI) have discrete and specific roles in monitoring progress towards the Health of the Nation mental illness targets and the implementation of the Community Care Act, which will contribute towards meeting these targets.

12.15 The role of the SSI towards SSDs is less directive. However SSI has specific responsibility for monitoring the use of the Mental Illness Specific Grant and powers of inspection of certain services.

References
BRITISH PSYCHOLOGICAL SOCIETY (1992) On advising purchasers. Leicester: BPS.
FALLOON, I.R.H. & FADDEN, G. (1993) Integrated mental health care. Cambridge: Cambridge University Press.
GLEAVE, R. & PECK, E. (1992) Images of the contracting process. *Journal of Mental Health,* **1,** 219-229.
GROVES, T. (1990) After the asylums: the local picture. *British Medical Journal,* **300,** 1128-1130.
HEALTH ADVISORY SERVICE (1993) A Unique Window on Change. Annual Report of the Director. London: HMSO.
HOOD, S. & WHITEHEAD,T. (August 1990) One path to a comprehensive District psychiatric service, *Health Services Management,* 174-7.
KNAPP, M. & BEECHAM, J. (1992) Costing mental health services. *Psychological Medicine,* **20, 4,** 893-908.
LAVENDER, A. & HOLLOWAY, F. (1988) Community Care in Practice. Chichester: Wiley.
MURPHY, E. (1991) After the asylums. London: Faber and Faber.
PECK, E. & SMITH, H. (1991) Contracting for mental health services. National Health Services Training Authority.
REED, J. & LOMAS, G. (1984) Psychiatric services in the community. London: Croom Helm.

CHAPTER 13

EVALUATING OUTCOMES AND DISSEMINATING INFORMATION

EVALUATING OUTCOMES AND DISSEMINATING INFORMATION

> **Action summary**
>
> **All NHS and SSD Managers**
>
> ▌ Agree criteria and establish mechanisms for evaluating measures to achieve targets.
>
> ▌ Establish mechanisms to publicise local strategies and progress towards targets.

The need for evaluation

13.1 Evaluation is necessary to understand whether and why particular initiatives are succeeding or failing. It will highlight areas where methods of health promotion and service provision need to be developed or changed and suggest strategies to achieve these changes. Managers will wish to evaluate the structure, process and outcome of each measure.

Criteria for evaluation

13.2 The following, based upon work by Shaw (see References), suggest criteria against which services can be evaluated:

appropriateness:

the service or procedure is what the population or individual actually needs.

equity:

a fair share for all the population according to their needs.

accessibility:

access to services is not compromised by undue limits of time, distance or information on user rights or the services available, nor by the services' characteristics, structure, ethos or referral system.

effectiveness:

achieving the intended benefit for the individual and for the population.

acceptability:

services are provided such as to satisfy the reasonable expectations of patients, providers and the community.

efficiency:

resources are applied to the maximum benefit of each service user without being to the detriment of another.

13.3 It is important to evaluate the quality of service delivery as well as quantitative aspects.

13.4 As with monitoring, independent evaluation carried out by users of services and voluntary organizations can provide useful insights.

13.5 Methods of evaluation will need to be agreed jointly with alliance partners.

Dissemination of information

13.6 DHAs, FHSAs and SSDs should work together to ensure that information is shared between managers, clinicians and social workers to ensure that staff understand the changes being implemented and have an opportunity to feed back information. The development of Community Care Plans in conjunction with Health of the Nation strategy formation can be an important way of making this happen. Managers will want to ensure staff, users and carers and the local population are informed of:

- the goals of the strategy

- the reasons for the strategy and the chosen targets

- progress towards the primary and local targets.

13.7 If the local population is going to work with the NHS and SSDs to achieve the targets set out in the Health of the Nation, it needs to be given full and accurate information. Public relations exercises which hide difficulties and problems will soon lead to distrust and undermine progress.

13.8 Similarly, informing alliance partners of any developments in implementing strategies for change will spread good ideas and enable partners to work more effectively with the NHS and SSDs to achieve the desired improvements in mental health and reductions in suicide rates.

13.9 Achievement of the primary targets will not be instantaneous. In particular, the poor information base and historic mismatching of resources to need in the provision of mental health services will need to be addressed before real progress can be made. An honest appraisal of the local situation should be made and disseminated.

13.10 In addition to forming alliances with local media to spread information, such as through regular editorial space in local newspapers (see chapter 4), managers may also wish to establish specific organs of communication both with the public and between alliance members.

References

CHARLWOOD, P. (1992) Managerial creativity and mental health services. *Journal of Mental Health*, **1,** 201-6.

CLIFFORD, P. *et al* (1989) Assuring quality in mental health services. London: Research & Development for Psychiatry/Free Association Books.

DEPARTMENT OF HEALTH SOCIAL SERVICES INSPECTORATE (1993). Developing quality standards for home support services. London: HMSO.

INSTITUTE OF HEALTH SERVICE MANAGERS (1991) Managing mental health services: Report of project group chaired by P. Charlwood. London: IHSM.

KING, D. (1991) Moving on from mental hospitals to community care. A case study of change in Exeter. London: Nuffield Provincial Hospitals Trust.

MCKEE, L. & PETTIGREW, A. (17 November 1988) Managing major change. *Health Services Journal*, 1358-60.

PECK, E. (1991) Power in the NHS: Case study of a unit considering NHS Trust status. *Health Services Management Research*, **4, 2,** 120-30.

SHAW, C. (1986) Introducing quality assurance. London: King's Fund Centre.

INDEX

Printed in the United Kingdom for HMSO
Dd 0301807   4/96   C10   65536   349113   12/34917